The
Duly Diligent
Stock Investor

Practical Principles for
Creating Your Own Fund of
Safe and Profitable Investments

The
Duly Diligent
Stock Investor

❧ ❦

Practical Principles for
Creating Your Own Fund of
Safe and Profitable Investments

Paul Wagner

D™

Duly Diligent Publishing, Inc.
Crystal Lake, Illinois
United States of America

dulydiligent.com

ISBN-13: 978-0-615708-71-3

ISBN-10: 0-615708-71-4

Book design by Greg Wagner

Grunt Work InfoDesign

CONTENTS

ABOUT THE AUTHOR

Paul Wagner grew up in Hastings, Nebraska and graduated from North Park College in Chicago with a degree in history. He served three years in the U.S. Army.

In 1997, at the age of 50 and after a 25-year career in commercial finance and factoring, he retired as a senior vice president of Heller Financial, Inc.

He and his wife Nancy currently enjoy country life in the rolling hills and hidden valleys of southwestern Wisconsin.

ACKNOWLEDGMENTS

I never planned to write a book about investing in stocks. It took me most of the 15 years since my retirement – after the dotcom bubble, 9/11 and the collapse in 2008 – just to convince myself I had been successful at it. Looking back, I came to realize that the analytical skills and discipline I had been paid to employ in my lending career had naturally flowed into my personal investing practices and had helped me succeed. I owe most of my investing success to the managers, lawyers and colleagues at Heller Financial, and in particular to the hundreds of Heller customers and clients I came to know who provided case study upon case study of both how to and how not to run a business. Thank you all.

I could not have left my career at the age of 50 with a plan to finance our future solely on the performance of our investments without the support of my wife, Nancy. Without her confidence in me and willingness to risk going over the proverbial cliff with me, I might still be taking the 7:10 train in the morning and the 6:30 train in the evening. Good heavens! Thank you, Nancy.

Unless my friend, Ron Richards, had confessed that he didn't read the Value Line reports he had paid good money for, I would not have convinced myself that a step-by-step introduction to the process of due diligence would be something he would read and benefit from. Now that I've written it, I expect him not only to read the book but to *do* it. In any event, thanks, Ron, for the inspiration.

My manuscript was never submitted to any publishing companies, so I'll never know how many rejection letters I would have received. Instead, I enlisted my family. My daughter, Lisa Bezella, served as my editor, which is why the book is so well-written! If you find any grammatical errors, laborious style or any other things of that nature to criticize, it's because I stubbornly overruled an edit here and there. Thank you, Lisa.

Thanks to Amazon's print on demand program, I turned over the formatting, design and publicity of the book to my son, Greg, whose resume includes publication production management for a professional organization. Greg has a company called Grunt Work InfoDesign and started his own publishing firm just to handle this book. You're reading the book because of Greg's contribution. Left to my own devices, the manuscript would still be a Word document on my hard drive. Thank you, Greg.

PREFACE

My good friend, Ron, gave me the inspiration for writing this book.

Ron and I have some things in common. We're both active seniors and retired. We were born in the same year, grew up in the same town in Nebraska and went to the same high school. But we went our separate ways after high school and our lives have been very different since.

Our careers were nothing alike. While I had a career focused almost entirely on providing financing to companies, Ron's work history was very diverse. He managed a bus terminal early on. He sold life insurance and mobile homes and real estate. For a time, he was a waterfowl hunting guide. His wife playfully accuses him of retiring at 35. It's not true, of course, and he still operates a transportation escort service for oversized loads of specialized freight.

Ron is an Outdoorsman, a word capitalized for the same reason that "Methodist" is capitalized. It defines his soul. He hunts and fishes, and when he's done he hunts and fishes some more. He shoots waterfowl and deer and antelope and pheasants and turkeys and doves. He shoots from a stand, a blind, a roadside or behind a bush. You might find him fishing from a big boat for little fish or from a little boat for big fish. He trolls, back trolls, casts and drifts. Some years back he managed to find time to write a novel, narrated by a decoy, of all things. It's true. I have an autographed copy.

I think Ron is a great Outdoorsman. He has a well-developed sense of responsibility about his sport, an ethic that he's thought long about and internalized. About fishing, he tells me that 10% of fishermen catch 90% of the fish and I believe he's part of that elite 10%. He thinks I'm a great investor. I'm not, but I am above average – so far. That simply means that I have created a bigger investment portfolio for myself over the past 15 years by making investments in individual companies than I would have if I had invested in the S&P 500, the "average."

A couple of years ago, Ron became frustrated with the performance of the mutual funds he and his wife owned. He wanted to create a portfolio of individual stocks but he had no experience doing it. Stock picking has worked well for me but not everyone wants to take on the responsibility of making their own investment decisions. I resisted the temptation to give Ron stock tips or advice but I did tell him a little about how stocks are bought and sold. I told him about low-cost discount brokerages that many individual investors use and the research resources they provide. I told him about Value Line, a publisher of stock analysis reports that I have used for many years with good results.

Ron opened a brokerage account and subscribed to Value Line. While I read and benefit from the reports, I have a feeling that those numbers, graphs and tables make his eyes hurt. Not long ago, Ron admitted he files the reports religiously but doesn't use them. I got the sense he could benefit from an introductory course in how to evaluate potential investments. I mentioned it to him and he agreed. This book is a result of that conversation.

I am not an investment advisor, nor am I a certified public accountant or certified financial analyst. But I have tried to shed some light on how I evaluate a business before I invest in it, for those of you who may think of yourselves as unsophisticated in financial matters and not "cut out" to make investment decisions. My intent in writing this book was to give you enough confidence to make a step in the direction of taking more responsibility for your financial well-being. In my opinion, nothing demonstrates taking responsibility for your financial well-being more than prudently investing some of your money in companies which have meaning to you, which you understand and find worthy of some of your investment dollars.

There is some work involved in being duly diligent when it comes to making investment decisions. But it's not hard work. Certainly not as hard as completing a *New York Times* crossword puzzle if you've never done one. And while the work involves some numbers, it doesn't require more than simple arithmetic that can be done on a $2.99 calculator. Finally, thanks to the internet, all the information you need is available free online.

Readers who hope to discover in this book a magic formula or a surefire system to make money in the stock market are going to be disappointed. And even though I took some shortcuts and had some good luck and made some money early in my investing career, this book doesn't cover the art of trading in stocks. This book is about investing as if you were buying a local business that you intend to own for a very long time and planning to participate in its profits forever.

Long-term investing is not the only way to make money in the stock market. It happens to be the way famous investor Warren Buffett has made his billions, while simultaneously making Omaha a city with more than its share of very rich families who invested along with him way back when. Market timing, frequent trading and technical trading work for some people, and there are plenty of books available that cover those strategies in depth. This isn't one of them.

I believe that the best businesses in the world are American corporations. More than any other group, American companies have made immense contributions to the living standards of people all over the world. Owning some shares in a great company makes me feel like I'm playing an important role in my country's economic life through a direct supportive connection to the companies I own. I could certainly have more spare time if I put all of my equity investment money into a passive index mutual fund or two. That would make me a virtual shareholder in a whole bunch of companies – good ones, bad ones and ugly ones alike. Personally, I prefer to be a shareholder in a relatively few of America's finest companies.

FULL DISCLOSURE

To help guide the reader through the screening and due diligence steps, the book uses a real company, Fossil, Inc., as an example. At the time of publication, the author owned shares in Fossil, Inc. The choice of Fossil, Inc. as a case study implies no recommendation as to its suitability as an investment.

INTRODUCTION

A little nibble

I bought my first shares of stock during the summer of 1968. I was 22, married less than a year, and my wife and I were expecting our first child. I was in my fifth undergraduate year at North Park College in Chicago, finishing up at night while working for Dun & Bradstreet as a credit reporter.

The Dun & Bradstreet job was a good introduction to learning how businesses work. My duties involved calling on an assigned group of small to medium sized businesses throughout Chicago and interviewing their owners. I was expected to convince the owners to share financial information about their businesses with me. That information went into the credit reports I wrote when I got back to the office and helped me assign credit ratings to those businesses. Dun & Bradstreet training gave me a basic understanding of business organizations, some financial analysis ability and – perhaps most important – an introduction to the entrepreneurial class.

At the same time, my good friend Jim was working at American National Bank and the two of us decided to become stock pickers. We each put about $250 into a joint brokerage account intending to add more to the account regularly. With our initial stake we bought a few shares in two companies, American National Bank of Chicago and Brunswick Corp. We bought American National because Jim worked there. I have no idea why we bought Brunswick. The popularity of bowling, perhaps? Beats me.

Our fund didn't exist for long. My draft board caught up with me a few months later, and with all my deferments used up by then, I was selected to become a soldier. My wife and son went to live with my in-laws in Omaha, so Jim and I sold our stock ("liquidated our portfolio" in finance speak) and off I went to the Army. I didn't buy another share of stock for over 20 years.

In 1973, after fulfilling my military obligation and working briefly as a credit analyst at a specialized credit reporting agency, I took a job with Walter E. Heller & Company (eventually known as Heller Financial, Inc.) in Chicago. My experiences at Heller over the next 25 years gave me a good understanding of the fundamentals of well-managed businesses and the traits of poorly managed ones. I also learned how to look for trouble in a company's financial condition.

My first job at Heller involved approving small lines of credit for mom and pop retail establishments in the furniture, carpet and apparel businesses. Over the course of my career, I researched and managed hundreds of credit relationships with retailers, manufacturers, importers and distributors. We financed thriving businesses, as well as turnarounds and acquisitions. Our borrowers were almost always either entrepreneurs or private equity groups. My responsibilities took me "deep in the weeds" in understanding financial reports and projections, and in evaluating the quality of a company's accounts receivable, inventory and fixed assets. I had the questionable privilege of working out of problem loans, liquidating assets, working with creditors' committees in bankruptcies and on and on.

Taking the bait

Around 1991, my wife and I tried out a new restaurant in Plano, Texas named *Macaroni Grill*. It was a weeknight, the place was packed and there was a line out the door. A nice young person put our name on a list and handed us a black gizmo that she said would vibrate as soon as they had a table ready for us. That was a first for us. The restaurant was laid out and appointed unlike any we had ever visited, with an open kitchen near the entrance and gallon bottles of wine all along the walls. The food, the service and the atmosphere made for a great evening. The next day, I opened a brokerage account and bought shares of the restaurant owner, Brinker International, for $12 each, based solely on intuition that a well-run restaurant like *Macaroni Grill* would be one I'd like to own. Despite not doing any due diligence, I was lucky to make some money as the stock price climbed past $35 over the next few years.

Around that same time, the share price of a Dallas-area company, DSC Communications, fell like a rock when its product was blamed for a big communications outage around Washington, D.C. The Dallas papers covered the story for a time, and then went quiet. Months after the event, I happened to drive by the company's headquarters in Plano and noticed the parking lot was full of cars. I'm not sure why I was surprised by that. Maybe I thought the company had just evaporated after the bad fortune a few months back. In any event, this time I did some research and verified that the company was hanging on and had apparently fixed the product issues. I intuitively felt that if what caused the stock price to collapse in the first place had been corrected, it was likely that the path was clear for the stock price to go up, not further down. I bought some shares at $3 each. Within a matter of weeks the stock price was up to $11 and then I sold all of my shares to guarantee my profit. That was a big mistake because I hadn't made the effort to really understand the fundamentals of the company; I sold everything and I sold too soon. By 1993, DSC shares were trading for over $60. I failed to appreciate the phenomenal amount of money that can be made if you can see a temporary setback for what it is, buy shares at a fire sale price and then hold on to your ownership at least until the stock price catches up with the real value of the company.

Isn't hindsight wonderful?

Swallowing the hook

Still, two casts, two hits and two in the boat were all that it took to hook me on stock picking. And I've been having fun and success doing it ever since.

CHAPTER 1

First, the Basic Basics

What "Stock" Is

Stock (or *capital stock*) is another word for "ownership of a corporation." The building at the corner of Wall and Broad streets in Manhattan could have been called the "New York Ownership Exchange Building" instead of the "New York Stock Exchange Building." If it had, a lot of the mystery in people's minds about Wall Street could have been avoided.

A corporation is an artificial person in a legal sense, having an identity separate and distinct from its owner or owners. A corporation can have one owner or millions of owners, and the owners can be real, living humans with opposable thumbs or they can be other legal beings such as trusts or estates. The owners can even be other corporations. If a majority of a corporation (Corporation A) is owned by another corporation (Corporation B), it is a *subsidiary* and Corporation B is its *parent*. Some corporations exist only to own other corporations. A corporation like that is called a *holding company*. Warren Buffett's company, Berkshire Hathaway, is a holding company...a really big one.

Corporations exist as a preferred form of business ownership for two main reasons:

1. A corporate structure limits the liability of its owners. The corporation can transact business, enter into contracts, and incur risks and debts on its own account. It can do all those things without putting its owners at risk, beyond the risk of losing their investment. That's a good thing.

2. A corporate structure makes it easy for an almost unlimited number of people to participate in the ownership of the business. A corporation's ownership is divided up among owners who each own one or more *shares* of ownership, or stock. A share is another word for *unit*. A unit represents $1/n^{th}$ of the company, n being the total number shares the corporation has issued to the owners.

A person who owns one share of McDonald's Corporation could say, "I own 1/1,230,218,300th of McDonald's Corporation." (Maybe one couldn't actually say that, but they could at least write it.) If I myself owned all 1,023,218,300 shares of McDonald's Corporation, I would say, "Yippee, I'm rich! I own McDonald's!" (I wish I did. I'd insist they put brats and Polish sausage on the menu. And beignets for breakfast. Drop 'em in the fryer basket. What could be easier? Or healthier?)

How Personal Wealth is Created

There are any number of ways for a person to acquire a measure of financial well-being, or wealth. Some involve luck, like being born into wealth, marrying into it or winning the lottery. Some involve activities that are illegal because they are harmful to society. But for most of us who are blessed with good health, there are two main, entirely legal strategies:

1. **Work for your money.**

   I just checked my thesaurus and it doesn't include "work" in the list of synonyms for "fun" but whether it's enjoyable or not, I consider work to be a moral duty. Work is one of two building blocks of an economically strong society. Your survival depends on your work or someone else's. Either you must work or someone else must work to produce enough to ensure his survival, with something left over for your survival.

   The output that results from a person's ability and willingness to work is his *production*. The level of a person's production, as it relates to the inputs of his time, training, practice, effort, etc., can be defined as his *productivity*. The material *standard of living* of a society is based on the productivity of its entire workforce. Productivity is enhanced partly by such things as improvements in the health, education, acquired skills and motivation of workers, along with their organization and methods (think Henry Ford and the assembly line).

Really big increases in productivity and, thus the standard of living, are based on the second building block of a strong economy: *capital*. Capital can be thought of as property, including money and physical assets such as buildings and machinery, purposefully employed in the production of goods or delivery of services. For example, capital is responsible in large measure for reducing the percentage of Americans needed to produce our food supply from about 70% to around 5% in little more than 100 years. The increased use of technologically advanced machinery (capital) has taken more people off the farm than any other single factor, and has provided improved storage and transportation capabilities, which has given us consumers more choices of what we can put on our tables throughout the year.

Finally, the efficiency of how capital is used helps determine how much progress the material standard of living a society will achieve or how well a business will perform.

By now you've figured out the second way you can produce wealth for yourself...

2. Be a capitalist.

As money comes in from your work, save some of that money because wealth isn't measured by how much you make but by how much you have. And after you have saved some in a safe place, put some at risk and invest it in a profitable enterprise. In other words, become a capitalist.

Simply put, a *capitalist* is one who puts at risk (*invests*) something of value (capital) in the interest of receiving back something of greater value in the future (*return on investment*). The something of value is cash and the something of greater value is more cash. In daily jargon, this process is often stated as "putting money to work." (There's that "work" thing again.) In short, capitalists are people who take financial risk in the interest of financial reward.

There are two main types of capitalists:

a. *Owner-operators*

You could buy a business or start your own, using some of your money and some money from other people (fellow capitalists), and through talent and hard work you may find success, make money and secure wealth for yourself and your family. That would make you an *entrepreneur.*

If you want to lead a dynamic life, serve your fellow citizens and provide opportunity to people who work in your business, then by all means be a very successful, very profitable entrepreneur. Please! Your country needs you! Successful entrepreneurs have been a factor, maybe the main factor, in creating the great economic machine that is the United States. In a free society, where the rule of law prevails and competition is encouraged, the entrepreneur class may well be the best vehicle for efficiently distributing capital there is.

An entrepreneur not only risks financial capital but also risks his or her own human capital, investing so-called "sweat equity" – the personal time, talent and hard work that don't show up on the company's financial records. An entrepreneur is motivated by a compelling drive for psychic rewards, like being her own boss and accomplishing something meaningful through her individual effort. Management classes teach that this drive is a result of an individual's need for self-actualization, or the need to "be all that you can be."

b. *Outside investors*

Outside investors are capitalists just as owner-operators are, except they don't run the day-to-day operations of a business. They don't supply human capital, just financial capital. There are all types of investors who play a myriad of roles, from a brother-in-law to a manager of a pension fund to a member of the Saudi royal family. Even if you can't be an owner-operator, as an outside investor you are still an important part of a company that serves your fellow citizens and provides opportunities to the people who work for it.

There are two main ways to support businesses with your capital: you might be a lender or creditor (a provider of **debt capital**) or a part-owner (a provider of *equity capital*).

A lender makes a loan of capital for an agreed upon length of time, under agreed upon terms for an agreed upon cost. For example, you could loan a company a sum of money for three years, payable in equal monthly installments with machinery and equipment pledged as collateral at an *interest rate* of 8%. Your reward for your risk is getting your money back and then some. As conditions for making the loan, you might require your borrower to give you some representations and assurances about his business and to make some promises about, for example, how the business will be run, what periodic information will be provided to you, and how any collateral the business may have pledged as security for the loan will be maintained.

Debt capital comes in a lot of shapes and sizes, hopefully satisfactorily accommodating both the objectives of the lender and the needs of the borrower. The principal advantages of debt to the lender is that his arrangement with the borrower gives him assurances of how much money he can expect to receive back from his investment, and when. If the borrower fails to come through on his end of the deal as agreed, an event of default is triggered, giving the lender the right to take certain actions to get his money back. In the event the borrower becomes insolvent and files bankruptcy, any money that ultimately can be obtained through the sale of the business or its assets is turned over to creditors in full before the owners receive anything at all. The risk to the lender is principally a *credit or insolvency* risk, the risk that the borrower will be unable to pay what was promised on the arranged schedule, if at all. This risk is mitigated to a certain degree by the rights of the lender as spelled out in the loan documents and by the size of the layer of equity capital that stands behind the lender in the event of insolvency.

There are ample opportunities for an investor to provide debt capital to companies. Many large companies borrow money from investors by issuing *bonds* which are made available through brokerages. Investing in bonds of corporations is a big topic and isn't covered in this book, though it is worth pointing out that many of the principles involved in evaluating a company's bonds, particularly those that apply to judging creditworthiness, are fundamental to the process I use when evaluating a company I want to own. That's because both bond investors and stock investors value their investments based on their expectations of getting their money back and then some.

To the borrower, the chief advantage of debt capital is that it provides a business with money but it normally doesn't diminish the owners' stake in the business. Debt capital provides a *lever* that, if properly used, raises the potential returns of the owners. On the other hand, debt capital involves deadlines which may require the company to turn over cash to the creditor at a time when it might not be plentiful or when the money could be better used for other purposes. These potentially competing interests can put pressure on the business to be managed more with an eye to satisfying creditors than in doing what would seem to be in the best interest of the owners.

A business that borrows money is said to use *leverage* and a business that borrows a lot of money, relative to the amount of money its equity investors have at risk, is said to be heavily leveraged. Taken together, the arrangement of the debt capital and equity capital of a company is referred to as its *capital structure*. Sometimes there are elements of debt and equity capital in the same financing arrangement. This overlap is often in the form of *convertible debt*, where the lender is given the option to convert outstanding debt from the company into stock of the company at a certain price.

The typical outside investor who provides equity capital bears more risk than a lender. Although he may have specific rights, including the right to vote for directors and the right to participate in the profits of the business in proportion to his ownership, the equity investor runs the risk of never getting any of his money back, even while the creditor is being repaid year after year.

If a corporation becomes *insolvent*, meaning it is unable to pay its obligations to employees and creditors on time, the ultimate result may be a *liquidation* of the business. Liquidation involves the sale of anything the company has of value, with the proceeds of the sale being distributed to those having a claim for money. Usually this is done under the supervision of a bankruptcy court. The various types of creditors, referred to as *classes*, receive a share of the liquidation proceeds in an *order of priority*. In liquidation, it is unlikely that equity holders will receive any money at all. This is because stockholders stand dead last in the order of priority behind everybody else who has any claim to payment from the company.

However, the big attraction of being an equity investor is that while there is greater risk, there is the potential for much greater reward. Unlike the creditor who is entitled to receive back only the amount specified in the loan agreements, there is no ceiling on how much reward an equity investor can get back on his investment. If the company is profitable, the equity investor has a right to a proportional share of the profits for as long as he has ownership in it. If those profits grow year after year, the equity investor participates in the growth. If the business is sold, the equity investor receives a proportionate share of the sale price. As a rule, investing in very successful companies as an equity investor will, over time, generate a greater reward for his greater risk, *provided that the price he paid for his investment was reasonable.*

CHAPTER 2

The Equity Investing Process

In my opinion, the best way for an individual to employ his or her capital is by buying stock in one or more companies whose equity investors acquire and dispose of their ownership interests on the major stock exchanges. There are over 6,500 companies to choose from in the United States. When you buy stock in a good company, you are supporting employment and a higher standard of living for your fellow citizens. You are a capitalist. And that's a good word.

Let's see how it's done...

There are three main ways of acquiring shares of stock in a public company:

1. **Getting stocks free.**

    This is usually done through gifts, inheritance, marriage or at work through grants of stock from your employer. Getting stock free is generally a good thing, so if someone offers you shares, take them. And say, "thank you."

2. **Buying shares in mutual funds.**

    This book is not about investing in mutual funds. I personally don't like investing in mutual funds but they may be right up your alley. If you have a 401(k) plan at work, you are probably limited to investing your hard-earned, company-matched dollars in mutual funds. If you have a financial advisor, he has probably sold you on the merits of mutual fund investing and the risks you run if you buy stock in individual companies. No doubt he has good reasons. His main reason might be that he makes more money if you buy mutual funds. It's like what somebody said about multivitamins, "Multivitamins are very good for you. Especially if you sell multivitamins." The same thing can be said about large quantities of hard liquor. Or, mutual funds.

Maybe your employer and the government and your financial advisor are like most Wall Streeters and CFAs (Certified Financial Analysts) and hedge fund managers who think you just don't have the smarts to be a part-owner in a few publicly-traded companies that you've picked yourself and that it is just way too risky. Perhaps they've convinced you of that, too. If so, they're probably right. Perhaps you should also let them decide if you want Coke or Pepsi, Bud or Coors, mustard or mayo, paper or plastic. Just kidding.

The mutual fund industry in the United States is huge. In August 2012, the Investment Company Institute reported that the combined assets of stock mutual funds in the United States as of June 30, 2012, amounted to $5.58 trillion. (That's $5,580,000,000,000.) And those assets were spread among 4,613 stock funds.

From the ici.org website:

> "The Investment Company Institute (ICI) is the national association of U.S. investment companies, including mutual funds, closed-end funds, exchange-traded funds (ETFs) and unit investment trusts (UITs). Members of ICI manage total assets of $13.1 trillion and serve more than 90 million shareholders."

In June 2012, we were blessed with a choice of 4,613 stock mutual funds in the United States. Considering there are only about 6,500 publicly-traded corporations in the country of significant size, that's a staggering number of funds! Which prompts me to ask, "how do you suppose that if a person doesn't have the smarts to pick a good company out of 6,500 available to invest in, she can be expected to have the smarts to pick the right mutual fund out of 4,613?"

Can you pick a mutual fund based on its track record? Not if you take seriously every fund's caveat that "past performance is no indicator of future results."

Can you pick a fund by who the fund's manager is? Well, that's a possibility but then again, managers come and go. The best ones might get promoted to another job or be reassigned to run another fund that hasn't been doing so well, or they might be recruited by another fund family or they might leave the company to start their own hedge fund, and you might be left with a manager that plays Minesweeper at his desk when he should be working. And even if you were sure the fund manager would be sticking around, do you have access to his performance appraisals or his college transcripts to help determine how smart he is? Just what level of *due diligence* – the process of evaluation and analysis one goes through to understand issues of risk – is available to you, if any? Is the stuff that is in the fund's prospectus enough for you to really evaluate a fund and anticipate what it is likely to do for you in the future?

Some experts have suggested that the best way to pick a mutual fund is to buy the ones with the lowest fees. Mutual fund companies have a variety of ways to charge fees. Taken together and expressed as a percentage of the value of your account, they are referred to as the fund's *expense ratio*. Investing in funds which have low expense ratios is the recommendation of the venerable John Bogle, founder of the mutual fund company, Vanguard. Vanguard is owned by the people who invest in its funds, making it a sort of mutual mutual fund company. Mr. Bogle's research has shown that the average *managed mutual fund* underperforms the broad stock market indexes like the S&P 500 Index. A managed mutual fund employs people who evaluate companies and sectors of the economy, along with economic trends and conditions, and invests actively according to the fund's investment philosophy based on its research and findings.

A mutual fund with a portfolio designed to produce the same results, up or down, as one of a number of stock indexes, is called an *index mutual fund*. Its decisions are based solely on changes in the underlying index, not on the judgments of people reviewing research. (A stock *index* is simply a statistical representation that mirrors the combined value of the stocks that it comprises. The S&P 500 Index covers 500 big companies. The Dow Jones Industrial Average is also an index which comprises the aggregate value of just 30 major U.S. corporations.) In that sense, an index fund is more of a *passive* fund than a managed fund. Index funds rely on computers which work cheap, don't drive company cars or command big bonuses, so their costs are much lower. It's no wonder that Bogle recommends investors own index mutual funds, and it's no surprise that Vanguard specializes in them.

Mr. Bogle shows that, among other reasons, the cost of mutual fund management is a major contributor to the underperformance of the average managed fund. Vanguard's index funds have expense ratios that average 0.21% compared to what Vanguard's website says is the mutual fund industry average of approximately 1.15%. That little percentage produces an astonishing number when you do some arithmetic. Remember that, as of June 2012, there were over $5 TRILLION invested in stock mutual funds. If the average expense ratio really is 1.15%, mutual fund investors must be forking over something like $61 BILLION to managers of their stock mutual funds. (Remember what was said about multivitamins?) Want a little perspective on how much $61 billion is? According to the Sunshine Review (sunshinereview.org), a non-profit organization dedicated to state and local government transparency, that's enough money to cover the combined 2011 budgets of the following state governments:

State	Budget Amount (in billions)
Colorado	$21.4
Kansas	14.2
Oklahoma	6.7
Iowa	5.6
South Dakota	4.3
North Dakota	4.1
Nebraska	3.4
Total	**$59.7**

With over a billion remaining for Wyoming.

So what if the mutual fund industry takes enough money out of investors' pockets every year to run several states in America's heartland? They have a big responsibility for managing people's money and they deserve to be compensated for it. Shouldn't they be able to make a profit?

I have nothing against profit. (Remember, I'm a capitalist.) And if folks want to fork over money to their mutual fund manager, I have no problem with that either. Your mutual fund company will reveal in its prospectus what the charges are and what you will have paid them over a period of time if certain things happen. But it seems to me that people should realize how significant the effect of the fees they're paying is having on the amount of wealth they can accumulate over time.

On August 1, 2012, Vanguard's website, vanguard.com, had a great illustration of the effect of management fees on what you get to keep. There was an interactive table that enabled one to create a hypothetical investment scenario. I took the bait and contrived a scenario where a fund with an expense ratio of 1.15% (about the average for stock funds) produced an average annual return of 7.0%. The calculation revealed how much money an investor with an initial investment of $10,000 would pay to the fund manager and how much profit he would keep for himself over time:

	Pay to Fund	Keep for Self
1 year	$121.65 (17.4%)	$578.35 (82.6%)
5 years	$779.37 (19.4%)	$3,246.14 (80.6%)
10 years	$2,125.48 (22.0%)	$7,546.03 (78.0%)
25 years	$13,494.32 (30.5%)	$30,780.00 (69.5%)
50 years	$128,269.38 (45.1%)	$156,300.87 (54.9%)

The prospectus for a big fund of a major fund company which has an expense ratio of 0.94% includes a table that reveals that if you invest $10,000 and the fund yields 5.0% per annum, you will pay the fund $1,155 over a 10-year period. That doesn't sound like much – a little less than 10 bucks a month on a $10,000 investment. What they don't do is give you a frame of reference for that amount.

As I understand their table, that 5% per annum return, over 10 years, will make your investment go from $10,000 to $15,513, for a gross profit of $5,513, or 55.13% of your original $10,000. Good for you. Of that, the fund will take $1,155, leaving you with a net profit of $4,358, or 43.58%, of your original investment. Not quite as good. The mutual fund's $1,155 take will be 11.55% of your original investment and 11.55/55.13, or **20.9% of your profit**. That's more than the 15% Uncle Sam will get on your long-term capital gains. People complain about tax rates! Between your friends at the mutual fund company and your favorite Uncle named Sam, you'll give up 32.8% of your profit. (The Federal government will get 15% of your $4,358 net profit, or $763.70 and your mutual fund will get $1,155 for a total of $1,808.70, or 32.8% of your gross profit.)

My parents stressed the importance of sharing but I think you can take that concept too far sometimes, don't you? Many companies pay stockholders cash every 3 months in the form of a *dividend*. The dividends of several companies amount to 5% or more of the market price of their stock. If you could find 4 financially sound companies who consistently paid 5% dividends, you could buy $2,500 worth of shares in each one and pay your discount broker just $64 to handle both the initial purchases and the sale of the shares 10 years later. Your investments would earn the same amount of money over 10 years as the hypothetical mutual fund, but you would keep $1,091 more of the profit. Your cost of $64 amounts to only 0.64% of your original investment, not the 11.55% the mutual fund would cost you. That seems to be a pretty reasonable amount of sharing, right? Of course, there's no guarantee that all of those 4 companies will continue to pay 5% dividends for 10 years. On the other hand, there's a chance some of those 4 companies will raise their dividend payments over the years. By the way, mutual funds don't guarantee their performance either.

When people tell you that you can't outperform your mutual fund, they're probably mistaken. This simple example shows that you start out with a huge cost advantage, because you're not paying the salaries and expenses of the fund manager or chipping in on the company holiday party.

There are probably a few mutual funds out there whose performance will justify the fees they charge. But, according to Bogle, the odds of you finding one of those are not all that good. If you are a mutual fund investor, you owe it to yourself to check your fund's performance over the past 10 years and compare it to what an index fund would have returned to you over the same period. You may find that your fund manager hasn't been earning the higher cost you've been paying for the manager's expertise.

3. Buying Into Good Companies You Like

Enough about mutual funds. You may be satisfied with your funds and may have no interest in changing the way you invest. You have lots of company. But if it's part of your nature to "do it yourself" in other areas of your life, I hope the rest of this book will show you how you can save money by investing in companies directly (in effect managing your own fund) and potentially beat the big players by playing a different game.

CHAPTER 3

Paul's Principles of Picking Stocks

1. Know Who You Are

2. Know What You Know

3. Know What You Don't Know

4. Use a Discount Broker

5. Know What You Want and Make a List

6. Do Due Diligence

7. Go Heavy on the Crème de la Crème

8. Don't Overpay

9. Diversify but Not Too Much

10. Keep Score and Be Patient

11. Stay Humble

I will discuss each of these principles at some length. You may be tempted to skip the discussion of the first three principles to jump ahead to the nuts and bolts. Don't do it. You paid for the whole book. Plus, the midterm will have questions on all of it.

Principle #1 – Know Who You Are

I won't use a lot of ink on this subject, which has been pretty well covered by Oprah and Dr. Phil, but before you start constructing your stock portfolio, you should ask yourself the following questions:

1. **How old am I?**

   Your stage of life will influence your time horizon for your financial goals. In general, the younger you are, the longer your time horizon; the longer your time horizon, the more risk you are willing to take. If you are older, protecting your nest egg may be your primary concern and you may be what the late Benjamin Graham, mentor of Warren Buffet, described as a *defensive* investor. If you are younger and ambitious, and are willing to treat investing as a sort of part-time job or small business, you might be what Graham called an *enterprising* investor. Whether defensive or enterprising, the key word is "investor." An investor is not a speculator or a trader betting which way the stock market is going to go from moment to moment; an investor is an owner. Wall Street exists for your convenience, enabling you to become an owner in companies (easily and cheaply) and to sell your ownership interest in your companies when you need to or feel you have something better to do with your money.

   No matter what your stage of life, nothing says you have to put all your money in stocks you pick or in mutual funds at all. Diversification is a key principle of prudent investing, and owning stocks, bonds and perhaps a little real estate is a sound strategy. If you're new to picking stocks yourself, you should feel no pressure to jump into the deep end head first. You can wade in the shallow end and build a portfolio one company at a time, while holding most of the stock portion of your investments in a low-cost index mutual fund until you find that great company you can buy at a great price.

2. How secure is my current income?

If you have a job that you feel secure in or if you have marketable job skills that have value in almost any economic environment, you will no doubt feel comfortable taking on more risk than you will if you feel uncertain about being able to maintain your current level of income. The same holds true for a retiree who is getting some combination of a secure monthly pension, annuity or Social Security benefits that are sufficient to provide for his reasonable needs for the foreseeable future.

3. How large is my stash o' cash?

Everyone needs a rainy day fund of some size to resort to in the event of an interruption in their cash flow, whether it is caused by a loss of income or by an unexpected demand for cash to fix or replace something that breaks. It happens. Again, the less secure your cash flow – in or out – the greater your need to put money away in a safe place. And the bigger your stash of cash, the more confidently you can put money into longer-term, higher yielding investments.

4. How well do I react when I screw up?

You are going to make mistakes. Almost every investment has the potential to be a mistake in at least some small sense. Despite your best efforts, you run the risk of paying too much for the wrong company, paying too much for the right company, selling too soon, selling too late. You can't duck reality.

The following quote is attributed to Erica Jong, author of *Fear of Flying*:

> *Take your life in your own hands, and what happens?*
> *A terrible thing: no one to blame.*

If you have a tendency to cry over spilled milk, you'd better get over it. If you kick the dog when you miss a shot from the blind, you need to see somebody – soon. Maybe you would be better off if you stuck with your mutual fund. Or you might want to finish this book and learn ways to minimize the number of mistakes you make and to mitigate the negative effects of those you do make.

5. **Is my partner on board with what I'm about to do?**

If there's a special person you share your life with, especially someone who wins when you win and loses when you lose, it's important that he or she be as committed as you are to making investments in companies through a stock broker.

Principle #2 – Know What You Know

Everybody's brain stores a huge amount of data and the way your particular brain interprets the data it stores is unique to you. Some of the data is potentially useful to you when it comes to investing your money and picking stocks. Every day you come into incidental contact with companies and your brain automatically receives and stores information about those companies, whether you are aware of it or not. For it to be useful to your investing goals, you just need to access the information and process it. That requires a new awareness.

You're coming into contact with publicly-owned companies daily. For starters:

In the shower, you lather up with Dove made by Unilever (UL) that you bought at Walgreens (WAG).

At breakfast, you scarf down cereal made by General Mills (GIS) that you bought at Safeway (SWY), while you watch Fox News Channel (NWSA) over your DirecTV (DTV) connection.

You hop into your Ford (F) and, on your way to the train, you stop at the automatic teller machine made by Diebold (DBD) outside Wells Fargo Bank (WFC). You grab a cup of coffee at Starbucks (SBUX). On the train, you use your Apple (AAPL) iPad to get market news from CNBC (Comcast-CMCSA) or sports news from ESPN (Disney-DIS) and to check your email at Yahoo! (YHOO).

That's a list of 14 companies you "know" compiled in a matter of minutes and we've left out a whole bunch of companies like your electric utility, the oil company and the refiner who fueled your Ford, the REIT that owns your apartment complex, the shoe company that imported your shoes and the retailer that sold you your belt.

You might not think you really know these companies but you have a good idea about what they do, how busy they seem to be, how much you like their product or service, and *how much you would miss them if they were gone*. If you feel you would miss the companies you do business with if they weren't around, then there are probably plenty of other folks like you who would feel the same way. If their product, service or location weren't attractive to you, or if you felt that another company in the same business would serve your needs just as well or better, then you probably wouldn't miss them if they went away.

In short, you have an innate sense of a company's value to you as a living organism. And if you start thinking about products and services in that sense, you'll be taking a first step towards identifying companies that you would like to own.

So, your first assignment is to pay attention to things you take for granted. Ask yourself:

- Who made this?

- How was this made?

- Why do I use this instead of something similar?

- How much would I miss this if I couldn't get it anymore?

This process may lead you to some great investment ideas, especially when you run across something new to you. You may remember me relating my *Macaroni Grill* moment, where a restaurant experience prompted me to make an investment in Brinker International. I didn't (and still don't) know how to run a restaurant but I knew enough about the restaurant business from being a frequent diner at all types of restaurants that I felt comfortable making an investment in one. I was lucky that it worked out and I definitely don't recommend investing based on gut feel instead of due diligence, but it is illustrative of the type of thought process and awareness I recommend you develop as a first step.

The second part of "knowing what you know" is to consider the possibility that you have some information about a company that isn't generally known to a less-aware public or even to the investment industry.

Caution: I'm not talking here about inside information that only the senior management or directors of the company might be expected to know. That kind of information is useless to you until it's been made public. If you were to buy or sell shares based on information like that, you would be a felon and you could go to jail. Don't be tempted.

The kind of information I'm talking about concerns things that are unlikely to be factored into the algorithms on Wall Street. The information may be about a small company that nobody on Wall Street seems to be paying attention to. Your awareness of things that fall under the headings of "new" or "different" or "better" or "more" gives you an advantage over an investor who doesn't notice things like that – probably a big advantage over many mutual fund managers. A new product, a new store concept, a new menu, a different method, a better solution…those things represent change and they should make you curious. A factory or a warehouse opening (or closing) can signal growth or, in the event of a closing, leaner operating dynamics.

Let's say you worked at a hospital a few years ago which had spent a million dollars on robotic surgery equipment that its surgeons say reduces the inherent risks of surgery and its hospital administration likes because it reduces the risk of lawsuits, you might have wanted to find out who makes it. That may have led you to invest in Intuitive Surgical (ISRG) when the price of a share of stock was $80. It's over $500 now (June 2012).

In our small town there is a trail on an old railroad bed. For many years the town has had a public campground along the trail with about a dozen sites under a grove of walnut trees. Nowadays the campground has about 30 sites filled with campers on weekends, almost all of them there to ride their ATVs on that trail and several other trails that connect with it. We moved to our home 15 years ago. Our house is just a quarter of a mile from the trail and when we first moved into it, we liked riding our bicycles on the trail. Back then, the trail was used by walkers, bike riders, horse riders and a few ATV riders. In the winter, snowmobiling was popular. Over the past few years though, trail use by ATVers has increased considerably to the point that few folks want to walk the trail or ride their bicycles on it anymore. The town has spent money to expand and improve the campground and talked the State into paying for the construction of a $400,000 trailside shower and restroom facility.

Campground fees have increased and yet the usage keeps increasing. It's been a real economic boon to the town. I'd like to be able to report that I made a connection between the surge in the popularity of riding ATVs on old railroad beds and the possibility that a manufacturer of ATVs would be a big beneficiary. I'd like to be able to say that my astute observation led me to make an investment in Polaris Industries (PII) back in 2000 when I could have bought a share for $9. Shares have traded over $80 in 2012. Yup, I'd like to be able to say those things but I can't because I didn't make that connection.

Principle #3 – Know What You Don't Know

Ignorance is not a four-letter word. Foolishness is. Ignorance can be remedied. Foolishness must be avoided. It is foolish not to admit your ignorance.

While your mere act of living is giving you more hints about picking stocks than you may have imagined, there's a lot more you need to know about a company than how much you like what it provides you. Your intuition is helpful only in making you curious about whether or not one of your favorite companies would make a good investment. It's a good place to start but risking your money on a hunch is a way of life in Las Vegas, not wise investing.

Remember, **when you buy stock, you're buying a company, not placing a bet**. It's helpful to think of a broker on Wall Street in the same way you think of a real estate broker who exists for your convenience. If you're in the market for real estate, you're probably going to seek out a realtor but you're unlikely to take his word that a particular condo or lake house is just right for you. You don't have a problem admitting you know absolutely nothing about the property until you've checked it out for yourself. It would be foolish not to.

So, before you start buying part-ownership in businesses, recognize that you don't know as much about them as you need to know. In short, don't assume you can spend less time deciding on what companies to invest your money in than you would spend deciding where to spend your winter vacation, which dress to buy for your daughter's wedding, or which wine to serve with rainbow trout amandine.

Getting the knowledge you need is going to require *due diligence*. Somewhere between here and the back of the book we're going to spend a rather lengthy chapter on due diligence. In my opinion, doing due diligence is not only necessary, it is educational and interesting at the same time.

Principle #4 – Use a Discount Broker

This is an important principle but my editor might think it's out of place here. If that's the case, you'll be reading this somewhere else.

I think the term "discount" broker is unfortunate and that "self-service" broker would be more descriptive, but I'll stick with convention and use "discount" broker to describe the type of brokerage that isn't a "full-service" broker.

Discount brokers and full-service brokers both charge you a fee when you buy and sell stocks through them. The fees of discount brokers are much lower than those of full-service brokers. That's reason enough for me to want to use a discount broker. There are a lot of discount brokers to choose from. Among them are TDAmeritrade, Scottrade, Fidelity, Schwab, Vanguard and several more. An online search will direct you to a number of different sources of ratings of discount brokers, including sites like smartmoney.com and consumersearch.com. It also can't hurt to visit the websites of the many brokers to see what they offer. A number of the larger institutions have offices in most cities, making information accessible and opening an account easy. Doing it by phone and online is simple, too.

All of the brokers mentioned are members of SIPC, which provides protection of your account balances in the same way the FDIC protects your bank accounts.

I've never used a full-service brokerage but my understanding is when you deal with a full-service brokerage, you actually deal with a person who used to be called a "broker," as in "salesperson," but is now called a "financial advisor."

Like mutual funds, financial advisors are perfect for some people. For me though, the two institutions present the same basic problem: there are thousands of them out there, so how would I know if I was picking the best one? And, to me at least, placing a bet on a single financial advisor who happens to have a winning smile and a charming bedside manner seems more like gambling with my money than owning a few of America's finest companies. At least if you made a mistake in your selection of a particular company to invest in, you can easily sell your ownership stake. It only takes a second or two, but it might be a bit more of a hassle to replace your advisor.

I recognize that financial advisors do a lot more for their clients than just handle stock market transactions. They provide valuable assistance to their clients in matters such as retirement planning, insurance, annuities, taxes and more. And, from what I can tell, they are really nice folks. By all means consider using a financial advisor for those things. But from my point of view, you should use a discount broker when it comes to building and managing the portfolio of companies that you own.

One thing that's really hard to tell by looking at their websites is how much it will cost you to do business with a financial advisor. I think you have to call and set up an appointment to find out. Based on the websites I've perused, they don't seem to want the general public to have that much information. That's not the case with the discount brokers. It's a very competitive business and discount brokers scream their commission schedules to anyone even mildly curious. I guess they consider their fees reasonable and therefore they're not reluctant to blurt them out to even a casual passerby. It's been a long time since I've paid even $10 to sell a whole bunch of shares, and like personal computers and big screen televisions, the prices seem to just keep going down.

The low price is not the only reason to go with discount brokers though. Executing stock transactions is only one of the benefits. They give you a lot more than just fast execution according to your instructions and the extra stuff is at no additional charge. A typical major discount broker will offer you the following tools and a lot more:

- Free research from multiple independent research firms

- In-depth stock screening tools: you input criteria you're looking for and the screener displays a list of companies that meet your criteria. Stock screening tools can be very helpful as you develop your *suspect list* – something we'll be covering in the next chapter.

- Detailed charts and graphs

- Real-time quotes

- Portfolio tracking and performance reporting

Principle #5 – Know What You Want and Make Lists

I'm not going to get all biz-school in this chapter and go into the whole "mission-goals-strategy-execution-tactics" process but you really should put some thought into what your objectives are before you get very far. If you're going to be serious about things, you should really write down what your goals, strategies and tactics are. And save what you've written so that you can refer back to it over and over.

If you are an enterprising investor and are drawn to stock picking as a challenge to see if you can do better than a mutual fund you've been in for years, or if you want to beat the S&P 500 Index, write that down. That's your goal.

If you want to be financially independent by the time you stop working, write it down. If you want the income you receive from your investments after you retire to fund a comfortable lifestyle for yourself and perhaps for your heirs, write it down. If you think the best way to do that is to make regular contributions to a self-directed IRA and to invest that money in safe, financially-stable companies who have a long history of paying dividends in good times and bad, write that tactic down. If you don't want to spend more than a few minutes a week investing, write that down too.

Going through the exercise of examining your goals, strategies and tactics while keeping in mind "who you are" is an important step in the stock picking process. Whatever your goals, there are strategies and tactics you can employ to reach those goals. With one caveat: *if your goal is to quit your job and strike it rich in the stock market by day trading your way to millions, you are going to fail.* You might be lucky and catch an epic wave on your way to some momentary profits but ultimately you're just going to put money in your broker's bank account.

Why do I emphasize writing it down and saving what you've written? Investing in stocks has some dynamics of a trip to the mall, the grocery store or Home Depot...especially Home Depot. I don't know about you but I almost always come back home with something that I didn't set out to buy and something that I don't need. And I must admit that there have been times when I've arrived at the grocery store and forgotten what I came for. That's why the CEO of my house has me take a list when I'm sent on a shopping errand.

If you've written down your carefully considered goals and strategies, you'll tend to stay focused and not wander from your objectives. That will increase the likelihood that the portfolio of investments that you develop will be pointed at the target you want to hit. There are a few thousand U.S. companies whose stock is traded on the exchanges. There is no shortage of stock picking ideas out there. You'll come up with some on your own based on your newly acquired awareness of what's around you. And if you read the business pages, use the resources at your broker's site, open your email box, or check into countless valuable sites like Motley Fool, Seeking Alpha and Yahoo!, there will be a lot more tempting ideas for you to consider. Just as you don't want to leave the grocery store with a cart full of items that were on someone else's shopping list, you don't want to buy a bunch of stocks that don't belong in your portfolio. So, focus.

Once you've been through this exercise, the very broad outlines of the kind of portfolio you create will begin to take shape. The companies you ultimately choose to buy will have meaning for you; you will know why you bought them and what you expect them to do for you.

Your Suspect List

The first step is to develop a list of *suspect* companies from which you will select the relatively few that you will end up owning. Your suspect list can be quite lengthy and the suspects on the list can be very diverse. Potential sources for identifying the companies that make your suspect list include

- **Your daily routine.** Earlier, I pointed out how your daily routine brings you into contact with the products and services of numerous companies whose ownership is owned by the public and potentially by you.

- **Your occupation.** The company you work for, its suppliers, customers or even its competitors might prove fertile ground for producing a great investment idea or two. You no doubt have a great deal of understanding about how some of these companies are doing, a firsthand knowledge of their product or services – perhaps enough to give you an edge over other investors.

- **Your hobbies or pastimes.** What you do when you're *not* working may have more meaning to you than your work. You may have intense passion for an outdoor sport like hunting, fishing, skiing or an indoor sport like casino gambling. Wouldn't it be wonderful if you could find an investment in a good company that provides products or services that make your activity more enjoyable and more satisfying? You surely have product or destination preferences based on your firsthand experiences which already give you a little information about the company behind them. That doesn't necessarily mean an investment in the company that provides your favorite product would be a good investment, but it might be and so you would be smart to put it on your suspect list.

- **The shopping mall.** I have a bias in favor of individual investors investing some of their money in retailers and the companies who supply their merchandise, or in restaurant chains, for a number of reasons. Most of the stores in a major shopping mall are operated by publicly-owned companies that you can own a piece of, and a trip to the shopping mall can provide fertile soil where you can dig up numerous candidates for your suspect list.

  There will be more discussion of this subject later in the book, but there are just a couple of reasons why I recommend individual investors consider the retail trade as a place not only to shop but also to invest. Although managing a chain of retail stores or restaurants is not easy and they can be risky enterprises, understanding the basics seems a little easier for most of us than, say, understanding the ins and outs of the steel business, the pharmaceutical business, or oil and gas exploration. Second, the premises and products of these businesses are readily accessible to us. We can even observe and talk directly with the company's employees and customers.

There are a host of other places to look for suspects. In one of my favorite movies from the 1980s, *Working Girl*, Melanie Griffith's character scored her big career coup as a result of an investment idea she got from reading the newspaper's society pages. Of course, that was just a movie but you get my point.

As you compile your suspect list, you'll want to determine if the companies you are interested in are publicly traded on the major stock exchanges. You can use the "Quotes" facility at sites like yahoo.com or your discount broker's website. At some sites, as you start to enter the name of the company, you will see a number of company names. Keep typing until you see your suspect's name and stock symbol, usually consisting of one to four capitalized letters. Make a note of the symbol.

Your Prospect List

Putting your suspects through a screening process will narrow your list to companies that meet certain criteria that you set. What you'll have left are a number of companies that will make up what I call a *prospect list*. How big your prospect list ends up to be will be influenced in part by what was on your suspect list but primarily by the criteria you've set for your investments. Before you start making a prospect list out of your suspect list, keep in mind that it's possible to set such rigid criteria that you eliminate every single company in the world.

A company that merits your investment should have the following characteristics:

- It should be **interesting** to you. You should have some connection to it and have some understanding of the business. If your understanding of it is fairly superficial, you should have an interest in understanding it better. It's not a requirement that you have esoteric knowledge of every aspect of the business but since you're going to be a proud part owner of it, you should be able to tell your partner, kid, or golf buddy enough about the company to assure them that you are investing your money in something you understand.

- It should be a **growing** company with sustainable profits. You cannot expect the value of your investment in your companies to grow very much over the long term unless your companies themselves are growing.

- It should be a business that makes efficient use of the capital you invest in it and rewards you and your fellow investors with a **premium rate of return**.

Screening your Suspects

Those basic characteristics are enough to start to *screen* or filter your suspect list to create your prospect list. One nice thing about investing in companies, as opposed to buying mutual funds, is that you can cherry-pick the universe of companies and you can be very picky.

Here's where the capabilities of your discount broker come into play. If you've chosen a large well-known discount broker, it's almost certain you will have access to sophisticated screening tools. They make it easy for you to determine which of the companies on your suspect list have been growing at a faster rate than the average publicly-owned company.

Websites like yahoo.com and money.msn.com also have free stock screening tools. I use the screening tools at fidelity.com without any issues and, as of this writing, Fidelity makes many of its screening tools available to folks who don't have an account with them. However, you can't save your screens unless you have a Fidelity account.

Screen #1 – Growth

The first objective of the screening process is to determine if the companies on your suspect list are growing faster than the benchmark I favor, the U.S. economy. The first screen will be concerned with the historical growth rates of two aspects of the company:

- **Growth in earnings per share.** The value of a company is more closely related to its future earnings and its cash flow than any other single factor. The minute-by-minute, hourly or daily changes in the market price of a company's stock don't reflect minute-by-minute changes in a company's earnings potential, of course. Think of a company you invest in as one you would buy 100% of (if you could) and leave your shares to loved ones. You would be most concerned with how much wealth and security the business could deliver to them over their lifetimes. You won't be able to buy all of a company but if you don't pay too much for the amount of ownership you are able to buy in a solid growing publicly-owned company, you can reasonably expect that the market will place a growing value on your company over the next 10 years as your company's profits grow over that same period.

- **Growth in the company's book value per share.** A company's *book value*, usually referred to as *stockholders' equity*, is a calculated value shown on the company's Balance Sheet and is simply the difference between the value of the assets on the Balance Sheet minus the amount of the liabilities on the Balance Sheet. Accounting regulations require that the assets on the company's Balance Sheet are valued at the *lower* of what they cost when they were acquired or their estimated current market value. Book Value *growth* is primarily determined by how much money the company makes, less how much it pays out to its stockholders; in other words, by the earnings it retains. With both earnings and the book value, you're interested in the "per share" values, because shares are what you will own.

Since I'm familiar with the Fidelity website and since you can access it too, I'll refer you to their website as one place you can screen your suspects for growth. (Hint: it would be a good idea to actually do this now instead of just reading about it. This is much easier to do than assembling almost anything that comes in a box that you open at Christmas.)

At fidelity.com, request a quote by entering a stock symbol, such as FOSL, the symbol for Fossil Inc., a growing company in the textile, apparel and luxury goods industry, traded on the New York Stock Exchange. (If you don't know the symbol for your suspect, enter the company name and Fidelity will help you find it.) From the quote screen you can obtain Research, which will include "key statistics" like historical growth rates. Note and record the several rates for Earnings per Share (EPS) and for Book Value per Share.

You are in charge of determining for yourself the growth rate that you demand from the companies you invest in – your *threshold rate* – but in order for them to make it onto your prospect list I recommend that the growth percentages for both earnings per share and book value per share should be positive numbers greater than about 5%. Why? The size of the U.S. economy over the period of good times from 1981 to 2008 (before the recent recession) grew at an average nominal annual rate of 5.78%. The growth rate is around 4% in 2012. You want your company to be growing at least as fast as the general economy. Ideally your company will also continue to grow faster than the economy in general during periods of very slow growth.

The economists and bureaucrats among us express the size of the U.S. economy in terms of the Gross Domestic Product (GDP), which is defined as the total market value of all goods and services produced in the U.S. in a year. Growth in GDP is stated in both *nominal* terms (without any consideration of inflation) and in *real* terms, where the year's growth rate is adjusted for inflation. In the paragraph above, I used the 5.78% rate, the nominal rate, in order to be consistent with the fact that historical company growth rates are not adjusted for inflation.

Compare the results of the screen you ran to your threshold rate. Our example, Fossil, passed the growth test of a minimum growth threshold of 5% over the past 5 years and over the most recent trailing twelve months (TTM) and is expected to continue to maintain a passing growth rate. If a company on your suspect list passes your growth threshold test, move it onto your prospect list. Repeat the easy steps above for each of your suspects.

That is all that you need to do as your first step in developing your prospect list. There's more to do but at least this first pass/fail step will narrow your suspect list to a more manageable prospect list by eliminating companies whose growth records are less than you require. Generally speaking, the higher your threshold growth rate, the smaller the number of companies that will end up on your prospect list.

When you've finished going through all your suspects, your prospect list should contain at least a dozen or so companies. You may not end up in investing in all of them, but ultimately you'll want to have your investments spread among at least four or five survivors, as it were, of a rigorous competition for your confidence – and your dollars. If none or just a very few of your suspects made the cut, it was no doubt for one of two reasons:

1. Your threshold growth rate was unrealistically high. You can adjust your threshold rate down, but not much below 5 per cent. If your threshold rate is extremely high, over 15% or so, you are going to come up with relatively few prospects. That's okay, but keep in mind that companies who have had extremely fast growth rates in the past are likely to have stock prices that already reflect that fact and make them expensive to buy now. (The concept of "expensive" will be discussed a bit later in the book.) Furthermore, they are certain to eventually have much slower growth rates and stock prices that reflect the slower growth outlook. Reality mercilessly puts limits on rates of growth, requiring ever larger quantities of growth just to maintain a steady rate of growth.

2. Your suspect list was full of slow-growth or no-growth companies. This will become apparent if you reduce your threshold rate down to the minimum of 5% and still none of your suspects pass the growth test. There are a number of factors that could have caused all your suspects to fail. Don't worry about why. There are ways to fix the situation. One way to create an alternate list of companies that do meet your growth thresholds is to hunt in the same industry or sector for similar companies that you like but passed over when you made your initial suspect list.

If you didn't get very many "passes" on your initial growth screen and are looking for names that will qualify for your prospect list, go back to fidelity.com (or another site where you can accomplish the same things) and begin a screen for companies that will meet your thresholds.

Like other stock screening tools, Fidelity's requires you to input your criteria in order to create a list of companies who meet or exceed the criteria you've set. To develop a list of companies who pass the 5% growth threshold test, the criteria would be

- Common stock, for "type of security."

- Earnings per share (EPS) growth greater than or equal to 5.0.

- Book Value per share growth greater than or equal to 5.0. **Note:** You may not be able to include the screen for Book Value at fidelity.com unless you are a Fidelity account holder.

- (*optional*) If you want to limit your search to companies in only certain sectors or industries, you can include additional criteria that will exclude companies outside your desired fields.

Screen #2 – Returns

For suspects who have survived your growth screening process, you now want to determine what kind of returns the company is generating. It's nice to know that the company made money and it's nice to know that each year the company made more than it made the previous year. But that's only part of the story: it's vital that you know how much effort and capital was required to earn that profit.

To illustrate, remember the "family business" concept that underlies your investment philosophy. Let's say you have a choice of buying one of two hardware stores in your town and each one shows a profit of $100,000 per year. You will favor Hardware Store A that has annual sales of $750,000 and exhibits a *return on sales* of about 13% (100/750) over Hardware Store B that has annual sales of $1,000,000 and exhibits a return on sales of just 10% (100/1,000). The number of hours you may have to work and the number of employees you may need in order to generate that extra $250,000 of sales for no extra profit would likely make the Hardware Store B acquisition an inferior deal to you.

The same logic says that if Hardware Store A requires a $300,000 investment in inventory to generate its profit of $100,000 (a 33.3% *return on assets*) and Hardware Store B requires an investment of $400,000 in inventory to earn the same amount (a 25% return on assets) you would be justified if you concluded again that Hardware Store A represents the better business opportunity.

It may well be that, as a consumer, you prefer shopping at Hardware Store B when you need a special fastener or electrical part, on the assumption that B's higher inventory may include a good stock of hard-to-find items that A can't be bothered with. But from an investment point of view, owning A appears to be the better opportunity.

This was a simple example to illustrate a point and things are never this simple, of course. But it does serve to illustrate that, all things being equal, investors will prefer a business that makes more money relative to the amount of money invested.

This example involved two similar businesses. Comparing the local hardware store with the local grocery store would have been like comparing hardware stores and grocery stores. That would not be a good thing because different types of businesses have different types of operating characteristics. For example, a well-run grocery store may produce a relatively tiny return on sales, while producing a decent a return on assets. The typical grocer operates in a highly-competitive environment where the customer is very sensitive to price and generates a *high volume of sales with comparatively little inventory* on hand – another way of saying that the grocery business is a high volume, fast turnover, low margin business. In contrast to a grocery store whose customers shop weekly or more often for rapidly consumed essentials, a hardware store caters to less frequent shoppers who come to the store looking for a variety of items with much longer useful lives, some of which are bought perhaps only once or twice in a lifetime – like hand tools, plumbing and electrical items and fasteners. While the customer may not buy the items a hardware store carries with much frequency, he usually buys them when he needs them and, like the shopper at the grocery store, expects the store to have them in stock. So, serving the customer requires the hardware store owner to carry a relatively large amount of inventory that turns more slowly than the grocer's. You can expect then that the hardware store is a relatively lower volume, slower turnover, higher margin business.

Considering the differences between the grocery store and the hardware store, it should be clear that while some ratios like return on sales and return on assets can be very meaningful when used to compare companies in similar businesses, they lose much of their usefulness when applied to different types of businesses. On the other hand, growth statistics have meaning no matter what type of businesses you're looking at.

Still, profitability must have context in order to be meaningful and the key return statistics that I recommend you use to screen your suspects are *return on owner's equity* (usually just termed *return on equity*) and *return on investment*. For initial screening purposes, return on owner's equity is just fine for leveling the playing field across different industries or businesses. No matter what business in town you might have an opportunity to buy, you have only so much of your own money to invest and, *all things equal*, you are most interested in knowing which business will return your investment to you fastest.

To determine your suspect's return on equity and return on investment ratios, you can return to fidelity.com, and using the same process that you used to determine EPS and Book Value growth rates, note and record the values for return on equity and return on investment.

In the context of return on investment, the word "investment" refers to owners' capital – stockholders' equity – plus lenders' capital – all the interest-bearing debt of the company. Recalling that debt serves as *leverage* to raise the return on owners' equity, you can expect return on equity to be higher than return on investment. A fair minimum threshold for return on investment is 10% and a fair minimum threshold for return on equity is 15%.

Exceptions, exceptions, always exceptions! Some companies have done almost all of their growing by buying other companies and have been successful at it. It can be a risky strategy if only because buying another company almost always involves paying more for the company than the current owners and lenders have invested in it. For example, if Company X delivers a return on investment of 10% and Company Y comes along and buys Company X for twice the total existing investment, Company Y can be expected to see a return of only 5% on its investment. Of course, Company Y intends to improve on that level of return through efficiencies it believes it can bring about. In general, though, a company whose growth is accomplished largely through acquisitions will have a sub-par return on investment, yet the stock market may reward it with a stock price that mirrors its earnings growth rate. By setting your threshold for return on investment rather high, it's possible you will miss an opportunity to invest in a company whose stock price will outperform the general market. It's just as likely that you will avoid making an investment in a company that represents a high potential for financial underperformance.

By this point, you should have a prospect list that includes companies that meet both your thresholds for growth and returns. At a minimum, the list should be limited to companies whose return on investment is at least 10%, return on equity is at least 15% and growth rate is at least 5%.

If the companies who made it onto your prospect list were houses, they would be houses that meet your minimum standards of, say, three bedrooms and a two-car garage. Now you want to go inspect them to check out the floor plan, the quality of the construction, the condition of the mechanicals, the nature of the neighborhood and the quality of the schools in the area before deciding which one to buy and how much to pay. Simply put, you are now ready to do due diligence…oh, hold on just a minute!

Screen #3 – Dividends

A lot of people don't want to own stock in a company that doesn't pay cash dividends to its stockholders every quarter. Paying dividends is not something I absolutely require of my companies; it is only a secondary consideration when I'm choosing a company to invest in. My primary consideration is whether or not the company *could* pay dividends. A company that can profitably reinvest a majority of its excess cash flow in its own operations and produce a premium return on that cash should ultimately reward its investors with a higher value for their ownership interest. America's most successful holding company, Warren Buffett's Berkshire Hathaway, has never paid a dividend.

Many companies, especially more mature companies with moderate growth rates, generate more cash than they need to finance their growth and so they pay dividends to their shareholders to invest as they see fit. Paying dividends is a perfectly appropriate way to return to stockholders a portion of their invested dollars as long as a company doesn't foolishly accumulate a risky amount of debt just to do so.

Many investors take advantage of a company's *dividend reinvestment program* whereby they can put the dividend dollars the company just paid them right back into more stock of the company without paying a commission. It's a smart thing to do if a person wants to own more of a company because it helps hold down the cost of investing. And because a dividend-paying company tends to schedule its payments at the same time each quarter without regard to market conditions, automatically reinvesting the dividends lets the investor *dollar cost average* his subsequent investments. That simply means that, over time, some reinvested dollars will buy stock when the share price is down and some when the price is up. When the stock price is down, the reinvested dollars will buy more shares and when the price is up the reinvested dollars will buy less shares. Over a long period of time this type of automatic investing can enhance total returns, provided, of course, that the company paying the dividend remains a strong growing company that can continue to pay the same amount of dividends quarter after quarter. Even better is a company whose dividends are raised from time to time. A lot of investment gurus recommend some form of a dollar cost averaging strategy for long-term investors, which is what you want to be, right?

In any event, if you insist that companies pay you a dividend every quarter you should screen your suspects to see if they pay dividends before you add them to your prospect list. You may also require that the amount of the dividend your company pays represents a certain *yield* on the amount of money you have invested. *Dividend yield* is simply the ratio of the sum of 4 quarterly dividends to the current share price. For example, a company paying a 25 cent dividend every quarter ($1.00 per year) and having a $25 share price today would have an annualized dividend yield of 4.0%.

Your threshold dividend yield rate is entirely up to you. There are a couple of relationships you should keep in mind when it comes to dividends.

- Typically, dividend yields on the stock of companies who are growing quickly are lower than on the stock of companies who are growing more slowly. One reason for that is the fact that fast growing companies are holding on to a higher percentage of their cash flow to finance their growth.

- A company's dividend yield may correlate to a company's financial condition. The stock price of a company who is struggling is apt to go down, sometimes dramatically. For a period of time, though, the company may continue to pay dividends of the same amount as when their stock price was higher. The yield therefore goes up. To illustrate: if the stock price of a company goes from $25.00 to $15.00 per share while maintaining a $1.00 annual dividend, the yield will increase from 4.0% ($1/$25) to 6.7% ($1/$15). The higher yield may not last long. Unless the company is successful at improving its operating performance, it is very probable that it will be forced to reduce the amount of its dividends or eliminate them entirely. A later section of the book will explain how to better understand a company's ability to pay its dividend at the current level.

- For the broad stock market, at least, dividend yields can be influenced by changes in market interest rates on government and corporate bonds. Some common stocks, such as the stocks of utility companies, fluctuate in price much the same way bonds do. When market interest rates go up, the market prices of bonds go down, and the prices of some stocks behave in much the same way. It's fair to say, however, that rising interest rates tend to put downward pressure on the prices of all stocks, dividend-paying or not.

To screen for dividends at the Fidelity website go to Research > Stocks > Symbol > Detailed Quote where you will find the Dividend Amount and the Annualized Dividend Yield. If the annualized dividend yield meets or exceeds your threshold, you can now add your suspect to your prospect list and get ready to…

Principle #6 – Do Due Diligence

Due diligence means basically the same thing as "adequate investigation" and it's commonly used in any number of areas of life to describe a process of evaluating risk. For example, before you pack up to go ice fishing you really should do sufficient due diligence to assure yourself that a) there's ice on the lake and b) it's thick enough to support your weight. The lengths you go to in determining the physical state of the water and how you relate your findings to the odds of your personal survival will say something about your risk tolerance and your wisdom. That's true about stock picking too.

If you follow some key principles, and proceed step by step, you can do an appropriate amount of due diligence in a reasonable amount of time right from your kitchen table. It's true that Wall Street is full of CPAs and CFAs and a host of other lettered analysts, forecasters and prognosticators, some of whom catch an early train to work in the morning and a late train home at night in order to slice and dice financial reports on companies. We can learn a lot from these professional analysts' forecasts, as long as we recognize that sometimes their forecasts don't cover periods of time much longer than your nightly weather forecast on TV.

Unfortunately, many of the professional analysts focus on predicting what a company's profit is going to be the next quarter, or what the market is going to do next week, or what the Fed chairman is going to say tomorrow. They work for the traders in our midst. I watch some of those folks on a particular cable TV channel almost every day. A few of them are amazing! They have so many opinions and sound so smart and talk so fast that I sometimes think they are on TV just to make folks like you and me feel dumb.

While I find shows on that channel entertaining and now and again informative, and while I get an occasional investment idea from watching, I almost never ever use any of the information or opinions or forecasts the guests on their shows put forth. Why? Because I'm an investor, not a trader. I am a part-owner in businesses I like. Simple as that. I am most interested in the fundamentals of the businesses I own and in information that instructs me about the business, its threats and opportunities, and its long term outlook.

Your due diligence should enable you to make an informed judgment about the company's future prospects and your willingness to consider committing some of your capital to the company's future.

These are the key areas your due diligence process should enlighten you about:

- The nature of the business operations

- Opportunities, risks and strategies

- The quality of management

- The sustainability of profitable growth

As you move through the list, your task will progress from basic knowledge gathering to analysis. I bring that up now only to assure you that by the time you're finished, you'll agree that:

- This doesn't have to be difficult.

- You will have de-mystified the term "fundamental analysis."

- You'll no longer be intimidated by the people who want you to think investment decisions should be left to people you pay to think for you.

You can obtain virtually all the information you need about these areas without cost. You can find free information about the company in the following locations:

- **On the company's website.** A major advantage the individual investor today has over her counterpart of just a couple of decades ago is the almost instantaneous access she has to company information, thanks to the internet. A visit to the company's website is very instructive, because the website now represents the most important vehicle the typical company uses to communicate its message to its customers.

- **The Securities and Exchange Commission (SEC)**, the Federal government's primary regulator of financial markets. The SEC requires listed companies to produce a variety of reports for its review and distribution to the public. The most important of the mandated reports to the SEC is the one called the *Form 10-K* report (don't ask, I have no idea why it's called that) a long and comprehensive report covering virtually every major facet of the company, including its audited financial statements for the most recent fiscal year. (Most companies close their books on December 31, but many companies close their books on a different month end. Whatever date they close their books, the financial reports in the 10-K cover one year, called their *fiscal year*). By law, companies must file their 10-K report within 60 days after the end of their fiscal year. SEC reports are instantaneously available online for free.

> When I started at Heller in 1973 and needed to get reports from the SEC, I was fortunate to be able to walk across the street to the SEC offices at the Dirksen Federal Building and ask to use their microfiche reader to peruse documents pertaining to a customer. And if I wanted to copy a report, I could pay to get a smudgy report printed by a dot matrix printer. It was nice to be able to get out of the office for an hour or so, but the process wasn't particularly easy.

- **Company press releases, presentations and conference calls with analysts and investors.** Companies release information about major developments and financial results to the media and to stockholders. Chief executive officers and chief finance officers of many corporations are invited to give live presentations about the company and its outlook at gatherings of analysts and financial reporters and investors. Telephone conference calls arranged to coincide with the release of quarterly financial reports are open to individual investors who can either call ahead to be included on the live call or listen later to an archive of the live call stored at the company's website.

- **Annual meetings of shareholders.** If you are already an owner of stock in the company you will receive an announcement and an invitation to attend the corporation's annual shareholders meeting. There is a vast difference from company to company in the format and scope of the annual meeting but that is where issues requiring shareholder approval are voted on. In actual practice, most votes are received by mail or electronically, in the form of *proxies*, in lieu of actual attendance.

- **Company visits.** I've never found it necessary to interview company officials at their offices in order to form an opinion of the company. But I do find it helpful, where possible, to connect with a retailer or restaurant operator by visiting one of their stores or by dining in one of their restaurants. In his book, *One Up on Wall Street*, the legendary Peter Lynch who ran Fidelity's Magellan Fund in the 1980s, tells of staying in three different LaQuinta Motor Inns on three business trips before investing in the company, and this was after having had a one-on-one meeting with the company's founder and CEO. If your prospect makes hand grenades, you might not want to go to where the product is used, but if your prospect makes or imports something that is sold at the mall, you really ought to plan a company visit to one of their retail outlets as part of your due diligence.

- **Outside research.** Most brokers, including discount brokers, provide access to research reports by certain analysts without charge. In addition, sites like Yahoo! Finance, MSN Money and a host of other online resources provide free information, analysis and opinion on companies and industries. Reference sections of some public libraries contain current Value Line reports that are otherwise sold on a subscription basis.

While outside research sources provide independent analyses of companies, much of the information they use in making their analysis comes from the companies themselves. In the vast majority of cases, companies are careful not to grossly misrepresent the information they distribute to the investing public, if for no other reason than to avoid being the star of a "perp walk" on the evening news. It's true that there have been a number of big cases where companies have deliberately misrepresented important information (think Enron and WorldCom, among others) and it's possible that managers at some companies are pulling the same kinds of shenanigans at this very moment. It's also true that accounting rules and regulations leave plenty of room for estimates and assumptions that can provide at least temporary cover for ill-intentioned or incompetent managers. Still, while the frauds make headlines, they are quite rare. Most executives and boards are honest, honorable, play by the rules, and run top-notch, trustworthy companies.

To help illustrate the due diligence process, I've chosen Fossil, Inc. (symbol FOSL) for a case study. If Fossil, Inc. was a company you had put on your suspect list, your screening process would have told you that its growth rate and return statistics greatly exceed the minimum thresholds, and you would no doubt have wanted to dig deeper and added it to your prospect list. I recommend you go through the process step by step.

1. Business Operations

Your due diligence examination of a prospect like Fossil should begin with obtaining an understanding of the company's

- **Products or services**, paying particular attention to things like the number of items in the product line, pricing, whether the items are necessary or discretionary, consumable or durable, high fashion or low fashion, finished product or component, high tech or low tech.

- **Customer base.** Individuals, retailers, wholesalers, manufacturers, governments. Number of customers. Size of market: broad or narrow niche? Selling process.

- **Geographic reach.** Where do they successfully sell their products or services – locally, regionally, nationally, internationally?

Besides being interesting and giving you something to impress your family, friends and neighbors with, knowledge of how your company does business gives you the ability to better understand its financial results. The attributes just listed affect, for just one example, the amount of assets required for the business to operate and those requirements in turn affect return on investment and return on equity – statistics you screened for in Screen Two. The operating characteristics also define the complexity of the business which affects the type of skills needed to run the business and the threats and opportunities the business enjoys, which have implications for profit margins.

Step #1 – The Company Website

Fossil's website is fossil.com. Put down the book now and go to the website. For now, stay away from the "Investor Relations" section of the website and just spend a leisurely five minutes at the "storefront," the part of the website directed to customers. Scribble down what you learned in those five minutes about Fossil, Inc. Then return to the book. (**Note:** This book was written in 2012 and, over time, companies change and so do their websites. By the time you read this, you may find that Fossil's website has changed a lot. In fact, I suspect it – and Fossil itself – will have. Still, the suggestion that you use a visit to a company's website to form an impression of the company's message is valid.)

Much can be learned about a company during even a brief visit to its website. As you discovered, without going past the storefront part of Fossil's site, the visitor can get a good sense of

- Type of products, breadth of product line and price points.

- Fossil's brand and image, or "personality."

- Scope and scale of operations.

A company's image is subjective, of course, but it should have one and Fossil seems to be stressing its image of fashion and quality. Did you notice the words "authentic" and "genuine" in its logo? Did you get a sense of the quality of Fossil's products? Was there a fit between the image you got of

Fossil's products and their prices? Finally, did you select COUNTRY or STORE LOCATOR from the top menu to discover that the company's products can be purchased in retail stores throughout the United States and in Europe, Asia, Australia and Africa?

A short visit to a company's website like the one you just made can help you form a lasting impression of the company. That is what the designer of the website intended. You want to know more about the company's operations, though, and often going back to the website will enable you to get it.

Let's return to the Fossil website and click the link to the ABOUT US page. First, read the "Company Profile." After you have read the entire profile, just for kicks, go back and look for the word "brand" (or some form of the word "brand") and count the number of times it appears. I counted 16 uses of the word. Do you think the company places a fair amount of importance on the concept of branding?

Although the company profile contains a lot of words, it really doesn't tell you too much more than what you learned from the pictures! When you read the first sentence, was there anything you found surprising? Anything you hadn't already inferred from your leisurely visit to the storefront? Anything in the second paragraph about the Fossil brand that was inconsistent with what you already knew? There is more complete information about the number of stores but we already knew about the international scope.

After reading the company profile once or twice you should be able to answer the following questions:

- Besides the Fossil brand, do you recognize other brand names carried by products created by Fossil? Do you think the diversity of brands is a positive attribute of Fossil's business?

- Does the description "high-margin profits" mesh with your initial impression of Fossil?

- What are three things Fossil believes have contributed to its success so far and are key to the future growth of its business?

Step #2 – The Form 10-K

The most important source of written information about a company's business is contained in the company's annual report, its *Form 10-K* (commonly referred to as *10-K report*) filed with the SEC. The report can be obtained at the SEC's website, sec.gov. Like most public corporations, Fossil's website provides a link to the appropriate SEC site where you can view a number of Fossil's SEC filings, including the 10-K report.

> To continue our case study, return to Fossil's website and to the Investor Relations page. Click on the link to "Stock & SEC Info"; under the "SEC Information" heading, click on "SEC Filings...." Those steps will take you to a page on the SEC website that contains a directory of Fossil documents. Filter those documents by typing "10-K" in the "Filing Type" box, and click on the "documents" button next to it to go to the "Filing Detail" page. Click on the 10-K link under the middle column heading "Document" to view the 10-K report for the most recent fiscal year.
>
> Some companies also make PDFs of its SEC filings available on its company website. Fossil has PDFs available for download in the "Investor Relations" section by clicking on the "Financials" link.
>
> This book uses Fossil's 10-K report for the year ended December 31, 2011, the most recent available.

After the title and the table of contents pages, the report goes into a lengthy and thorough description of the business. I recommend you spend a fair amount of time on this section so that you have a good understanding of the company's business. This part of your due diligence goes hand in hand with a basic understanding of financial concepts as equally important aspects of the stock picking process.

Part I Item 1 of every 10-K report covers a company's business operations in detail. Companies vary in how much and how detailed the information they provide, but each company is required to explain the nature of its business in terms of what it sells, who it sells to, how it sells, where it sells, and who its competitors are. Any major changes in the company's operations, such as selling off part of the company or buying other companies are required to be disclosed. Reading this part of the 10-K report will give you a much deeper understanding of your prospect's business than your website visit gave you.

Fossil packs a lot of information about its business into its 10-K report. Part I of the Fossil report is lengthier and more comprehensive than what you will find in the reports of many of the companies you will have on your prospect list. As you read the Fossil report, make particular note of the following attributes: (**Note:** I suggest you take notes as you read the report on your screen, but because it's so long you might benefit by printing the 20 pages of Item 1 and using a highlighter or making notes in the margins.)

- Product

  - How they buy

  - How they get the merchandise to the customer

- Sales breakdown by

  - Sales to retail stores/sales to consumers

    · Major retailers who sell Fossil products

    · What credit terms they give to their retail store customers

  - Product lines

  - U.S./International

The above attributes are more than just "nice to know" about Fossil or about the companies on your prospect list. Whatever company you perform due diligence on and no matter how complex their operations, take time to learn what the basic processes of the business are. They are relevant to getting a sense of what investments are required to support the operations, the risks involved and the opportunities for future growth. Ultimately, what we learn should help us form some conclusions about the sustainability of the company's growth.

Step #3 – Company Visit

This would be a good time to take a break and make a visit to one of your prospect's facilities if it's feasible. You have two options: visit a Fossil store or visit a retail store that sells Fossil products. A visit to either place can help you make a real connection to the company. You have an opportunity to ask store employees about how well the Fossil items are currently selling, popular items, comparable products of competitors, and frequency of returns. You can see for yourself the freshness of the inventory and especially, at a Fossil store, how knowledgeable and helpful the employees are. A company visit isn't absolutely critical to the due diligence process. It's more like icing on the cake, but if you have an opportunity to see the company's operations up close, you should take advantage of it.

The three steps outlined: time spent at the website, reading about the operations in the 10-K report and a company visit should give you an excellent understanding of your prospect's business. Many types of operations are more complex than Fossil's, of course, and you may think you won't be able to understand how some companies work. You're absolutely right. You should avoid investing in businesses you don't understand. Keeping it simple is a good principle to adhere to for beginners as well as for seasoned investors. There are plenty of opportunities to invest in companies that are well within your capacity to comprehend. Still, as in all areas of life, don't be afraid to expand your horizons. Learn as much as you can about as many types of companies that interest you, but invest only in those you feel you have come to understand.

2. Opportunities, Risks and Strategies

All forms of investing are based on a vision of the future. Whether you are investing in a home, artwork, bonds, stocks, a college education or a Caribbean cruise, your investment decision is based on at least a vague vision of what the future will be like. The fact that the future is ultimately unknowable doesn't mean that it can't be predicted with some level of confidence.

Every company has a future, of course, and management's job is to influence the company's future in a positive way. For a company to have made it onto your prospect list it must have performed well in the recent past, and now you are in the process of coming to a conclusion about the likelihood of it continuing that kind of performance over the next several years. Your goal is to acquire a satisfactory level of confidence in the company's future to justify investing some of your money in it.

To get a sense of the opportunities, risks and strategies of your prospect, you have the same resources available to you that you used to gain an understanding of its business operations: the SEC reports (particularly the 10-K, Part I), company press releases, presentations and conference calls, the annual meeting of shareholders, company visits and outside research.

A quick note about the 10-K, Part I: To varying degrees companies devote a portion of this part of the 10-K to a thorough outline of the risks the company faces, including the risks associated with being sued.

While you should pay attention to the discussion of risks, be careful not to lose a sense of perspective as you go through the list in the 10-K. There is a "CYA" (I think that stands for Cover Your Abs) element to this part of the report and the language in a 10-K discussion of risk can scare you so much that you avoid investing in a really good business. (It's kind of like the recitation of precautions that takes up most of the TV commercials for prescription drugs.) That's not to say that you should disregard the warnings, because while some of the risks may be remote they do exist and you should be aware of them. It might be helpful for you to read the 10-K discussion of risk for five or six companies to give you some context. When it comes to litigation, it's unlikely you'll be able to predict either an outcome or the impact of a negative outcome of a piece of litigation. You're left to the representations of management about the subject. We live in a society where lawsuits seem to be a way of life and, particularly in industries like technology, legal fights over patents is common. Problems with Federal government regulatory agencies, like the SEC, are a different matter. Fortunately, they don't appear often but when they do they can be serious. Highly-regulated industries like healthcare, finance and communications are more susceptible to governmental investigations and actions.

This is a good time to bring up the concept of *economic moat*. We can thank Omaha investor Warren Buffett for coining the term to describe the *enduring* advantages one company has over its competitors. The term is a metaphor that refers to the tactic of digging a ditch around a medieval castle and filling it with water in order to make it difficult for the bad guys to get inside the castle and make life unpleasant for the lords and ladies. When building the moat, it was important to make it deep enough and wide enough to be effective. After it was built, it was critical that it be kept filled with water. Otherwise, the bad guys might find their way into the castle and carry away the damsels.

As Buffett pointed out, the most successful companies have deep and wide economic moats that help them *sustain* their businesses over long periods of time. Castles with deep and wide moats made attractive places for lords and ladies to call home and businesses with big moats make attractive places to invest your money.

Examples of economic moats include patents, brands, exclusive rights, cost advantage, scale and customer intimacy (of a sort). The following examples are illustrative of the moat concept:

- **Patents.** A patent on the best drug for a particular ailment provides a temporary moat to the owner of the patent until the patent expires or until a better drug is developed.

- **Brands.** A popular brand minimizes some of the perception of risk of buying a product. Brands with loyal followings include Coke and Harley Davidson and Apple. Some Harley owners tattoo the logo on their bodies – that's loyalty and intimacy! Brands are important, but not because the brands create the moat and give value to the company. It is the track record of meeting and exceeding the expectations of its customers that the company has established and maintained – enhanced by a consistent reinforcing message of that track record – that gives value to the brand.

- **Separation anxiety and limited competition.** I get my TV signal from DirecTV because I live in the country, beyond the wires of cable providers. I could switch to Dish Network, I suppose, but it would be a pain, so I prefer to just stay put. DirecTV enjoys the fact that there is only one other satellite provider to compete with. Once they got my business they were likely to stay my sole provider simply because I don't want to put up with the hassle of leaving them. Those two attributes – limited competition and customer dread of the process of leaving – combine to make for at least a shallow moat. DirecTV has to keep its moat filled with water by giving me reliable reception, plenty of good programming and good service at an affordable price. Unless it slips up pretty bad, I'll probably be a good customer as long as I live where I do.

As you conduct due diligence to learn about your prospects' strengths and weaknesses, see if you identify any with an economic moat. What about Fossil? As you work through your due diligence on Fossil by reading its 10-K report, write down what you feel are its major strengths and whether any of them would fit the description of a deep and wide moat, a shallow and narrow moat, or no moat at all. If you intend to be a long-term investor, you should invest in companies that have sustainable advantages.

You also want to know what management is thinking about the company's potential and how it is going to continue to be a successful growing company. There are two main growth strategies available to companies: *organic growth* and *growth through acquisition*.

Organic growth is growth of the existing business through improvements in the product line and through growing the customer base.

Organic growth uses *processes* to grow the business. A company makes incremental investments in major processes like research and development, product development, and marketing and sales in order to improve the company's competitiveness and to provide more value to customers. Ideally, the money needed for the incremental investments can be provided by the cash flow produced by the company's operations, but very rapid growth may need to be supplemented by outside borrowings.

A strategy of organic growth serves companies who have sufficient internal capacity in terms of management, infrastructure and access to money to finance and manage expansion. Organic growth which proceeds in a deliberate, intelligent and orderly way usually poses a relatively low level of risk to the company.

Growth through acquisition involves buying other companies or parts of other companies. Companies have a host of purposes for buying other businesses: to quickly expand the product line, to diversify, and to expand geographical reach are just some examples. The capital required for acquisitions may be provided by cash flow from operations, issuing company stock to the sellers, taking on long-term debt or some combination of those options.

A strategy of growth through acquisition has the potential to produce "chunks" of growth more quickly than organic growth, but this kind of growth strategy is not without a fair amount of risk, especially for younger and smaller companies. To start, the due diligence process of evaluating another business has the potential for error. It is more difficult to understand the problems that exist in another company than to comprehend those in one's own company. Management might underestimate the risks or overstate the potential of the acquisition and end up paying too much.

Even when everything involved in evaluating the business to be acquired and structuring the purchase is done well, there are things that can go wrong after the deal is closed. There is a very real risk that the process of integrating the new business into the existing business will not go smoothly. Cost savings that may have been expected may never be realized. For a number of reasons, the acquisition may end up reducing earnings per share instead of increasing them.

If your prospect is a large company with a record of successfully acquiring business, it no doubt has learned how to mitigate the risks. Younger and smaller companies can do a good job of acquisitions too, particularly if they make relatively small acquisitions of companies in their industry.

This would be a good time to put down the book and go back to Fossil's 10-K report and read Part I again, concentrating on Fossil's strategies to build its business. Also, at the Investor Relations page at the company website, read the most recent letter to shareholders which is contained in their **Annual Report**. (The 10-K is also considered an annual report but many companies prepare an additional, traditional Annual Report, often on glossy paper with lots of pictures.) Their conference calls are also available at the website. Take time to listen in on the most recent conference call. (Yes, I know conference calls can be long, but you can multitask, can't you?)

When you're finished, record your understanding of what Fossil sees as opportunities for growth and what strategies they are employing. Then pat yourself on the back: you've already done more due diligence on a company than the great majority of investors do and you've learned a lot. We have one more non-financial aspect of the company to discuss before we try to analyze the implications of what we've learned

3. The Quality of Management

It would be great if you could sit down and interview the key managers of your business before you decided to invest your first dollar. You would be able to get answers to your questions about the managers' integrity, competence and motivation. On the other hand, you have probably been misled by someone you have met in person. That's why when people apply for a job or hire someone to do a job, references are an important requirement. Chances are you'll never meet the operators of the companies you invest in but you can make an informed judgment about them anyway.

First, though, you should know what you want from your managers. If you made a list of the traits you're looking for in a CEO, it would probably contain the following:

- **Passionate about the company's business.** A love of the business drives a CEO to commit the mental energy, creativity and time needed to see opportunities, to understand the competitive landscape and to infect his company's culture with his passion – in other words, to lead with vision.

- **Committed to the stockholders.** A CEO's job is primarily one of allocating resources – financial and human. Putting the interests of stockholders ahead of personal ambition results in making investments with an eye to sustaining the growth of the business – and the wealth of shareholders – over the long term, even when making the annual bonus numbers may be at risk.

- **Open and honest.** A passion for transparency and integrity will prevent the CEO from concealing problems, breaking rules or mistreating employees, will keep the company out of trouble with regulators, and will enhance credibility with stock market analysts and the investor community in general.

- **Effective.** Here's where management's skill, intelligence and a facility for communication come in. Not all passionate, committed, honest managers will be successful in "making their numbers" and if they make too many mistakes, the business will suffer. As an investor with a multitude of investment options, you want your manager to produce the kind of consistent financial results that will enable you to make your own "numbers." It may take quite a while for the mistakes of an ineffective manager to show up in the financial statements.

You can find information about the CEO and other executive officers and board members in company documents, particularly in the 10-K report and in the company's *proxy statement*, which is issued in advance of the company's annual meeting of shareholders and made available on the company's website. The proxy statement can also be obtained from the SEC. In these documents, you will learn about the length of time the key officers have been with the company and what positions they have held with the company and other companies. This information will help you assess the CEO's level of experience in the kind of business he or she is running. Importantly, if the CEO has been in charge of the company for a number of years and has produced the kind of growth and returns that meet or exceed your thresholds, you can be fairly confident that he or she is an effective manager.

You can sometimes get a sense of the intangible qualities of a CEO, including their openness and honesty, by listening to the conference calls, reading their annual letters to shareholders and by attending a shareholders' meeting if it is close by and convenient for you.

One more thing about CEOs: They tend to make a lot of money. So do professional athletes and Hollywood entertainers. More power to all of them, if they provide value in proportion to their compensation. I'm sure a lot of CEOs are overpaid. I don't know how much is too much but somewhere well into the 8-figure range of numbers ($10,000,000 or more) is where I start to scratch my head, even if the company is a really big one. If the company is of relatively modest size, my head starts to itch at a much lower number. If it's so high that I start to question the board's competence or independence, I'm likely to pass on the opportunity to invest in the company.

Ideally, your prospect company should have a compensation plan for its CEO and executive officers that appropriately compensates them for their results. It's hard to judge a compensation plan but if you're interested, the compensation plan and the actual compensation of CEO and other principal officers for the preceding year are disclosed in the proxy statement. You're not expected to critique the plan but you are certainly entitled to form an opinion about the total annual compensation relative to the company's results.

> The following note in Fossil's proxy statement of April 2012 is striking, and might be a confidence booster to someone considering making an investment in Fossil:
>
> > "*(6) Mr. Kartsotis* [Fossil's CEO] *refused all forms of compensation for fiscal years 2009, 2010 and 2011. Mr. Kartsotis is one of the initial investors in the Company and expressed his belief that his primary compensation is met by continuing to drive stock price growth.*"

Until now, your due diligence process has been concerned with fact finding. You should have a real good understanding by now of your prospect – the what, how and who of its operations. I picked Fossil because it has been a company with strong growth and excellent return on investment up until 2012. From this point, your due diligence seeks to lead you to a conclusion about the sustainability of those dynamics.

4. The Sustainability of Profitable Growth

Warning: you are about to enter a section that deals with *financial analysis*. I know it sounds scary, particularly if you have trouble making a budget, doing your income taxes or balancing your checkbook. If you feel you're not good with numbers and if just the thought of doing arithmetic on a calculator raises your blood pressure, you might be tempted to tell yourself that you wasted your money on this book and decide to donate it to your public library. Not so fast, please.

You *can* do this and since you have paid my publisher for this book, it would be a shame for you to put it down and walk away just when you're about to get your money's worth – and more. Take one step at a time. I assure you, only simple, 4th grade arithmetic – nothing more than simple addition, subtraction, division and multiplication – will be asked of you. A $2.99 calculator or the one on your computer will suffice. Promise.

One more thing: my publisher is providing free worksheets at dulydiligent.com that are intended to help you record the calculations you'll be doing as you perform your financial due diligence.

The ability of your prospect to grow its earnings or book value per share or to maintain its rates of return on capital or equity depends on numerous variables, some of which are controllable by management and some of which are largely influenced by what's happening in the national and international economy – over which management has no control.

Since predicting what's going to happen in the world economy is way beyond my level of comprehension or the level of comprehension of professional economists, I won't go beyond the following observations:

- Economic conditions can influence a company's results but not all companies are affected equally by the changing economic "weather." Companies that tend to be affected in relatively greater measure by economic conditions are considered *cyclical*. When the economy is sluggish, cyclical companies are likely to be unable to grow or to sustain their returns on investment or equity. Their earnings are inconsistent and difficult to predict. It is a challenge for some cyclical companies just to stay solvent until economic activity improves. When conditions improve, highly cyclical companies usually experience a major rebound in their operating performance, while less cyclical companies who were not as adversely affected by the slowdown in the first place show more modest improvement in their profits.

- A company's annual sales cannot *indefinitely* grow faster than the economy or the gross domestic product grows. A company that always grew faster than the economy would eventually (after a very long time!) BE the economy and be left with nothing to grow faster than! There was a time back in the late 1980s when Walmart was growing so fast that someone facetiously forecast it to do just that by a not-so-distant date. That can't happen. A company can grow faster than the economy for a long while though.

- Unless a company has a very deep and a very wide moat, it is unlikely to be able to produce premium rates of return forever. Highly successful companies invite competition and competition tends to drain moats; as that happens, stellar rates of return tend to come down out of the clouds and end up as more average rates of return.

Understand that whatever growth trajectory a company is on, that trajectory is likely to flatten out over time. Keeping that in mind, the purpose of your due diligence is to give you a basis for making a prediction about your prospect's future, even though some part of that future depends on circumstances over which the company has no control. Accept the fact that your predictions may turn out wrong to one degree or another. So will those of every other analyst. There's a fair amount of subjectivity involved in coming to your conclusions, but a lot less than if you hadn't put in the effort that you already have. Remember, human brains are pretty good at making subjective evaluations or else we humans wouldn't have survived as a species.

The remainder of this chapter is going to help you evaluate the following attributes of your prospect. You want to understand these attributes because if all of these attributes are positive and steady or improving, your confidence in the company's ability to sustain its profitable growth over the medium to long term is justified. If a company can sustain its profitable growth, its value is likely to also grow. On the other hand, deterioration in any of these attributes, *if it continues*, would suggest caution is warranted.

- Market Demand and Acceptance

- Efficiency and Liquidity

- Solvency and Sustainability

The financial statements provide the most objective tool for measuring these attributes. The 10-Ks and 10-Qs from your prospect's website or from the SEC provide the complete statements, which is where all the numbers and ratios originate.

Financial information is contained in Part II of the 10-K report; the 10-Q report presents the financial results for the recently ended fiscal quarter. (You can get some of the statistics you will be using in your financial analysis from the same online sources – like your broker's or money.msn.com or yahoo.com, for example – that you accessed to do your initial screen for growth rates, returns and dividends.)

I'll point it out here and it will come up several more times: the relationships you uncover through your due diligence are most instructive when one company's ratios are compared to those of other similar companies and when the company's ratios from one reporting period are compared to prior reporting periods.

Market Demand and Acceptance

By this point in your due diligence process, you have learned much about your prospect's products, markets and strategies. The financial statements can reveal much about how the company's offerings are being accepted by customers in its markets.

Two items from the company's Income Statements are helpful in this regard:

1. **Net Sales** represent the company's revenues, net of any customer returns or allowances. The trend in a company's sales suggests the trend either in the market or in the company's share of the market, or both. For example, let's say Ford's sales of vehicles increase steadily over a 3-year period. The increase might result from an improvement in the overall U.S. market for vehicles or perhaps from a better lineup of Ford models that appeal to more vehicle buyers than some competitors' vehicles. If Ford's vehicles are judged by customers to be a better value, then Ford's share of the market will tend to increase. You can get management's explanation for changes in the company's sales – and virtually all its financial statistics – in the "management's discussion" portion of Section II of the 10-K report and in the commentary contained in the 10-Q report. You can also learn a lot by listening to the conference calls that generally take place on the same day that the company releases its financial statements.

   Why is it important for you to get management's story about the numbers? Because it is your company and you have made a serious investment in it! You don't want to react like a bunch of nervous Wall Street traders who are notorious for their tendency to overreact to any news item, especially quarterly financial reports. Sometimes their overreaction creates an opportunity for you to buy stock at an attractive price. If you have invested in a company with open and honest and capable management, you will usually get information from them that will help you decide for yourself how significant the news is.

2. **Gross Profit** is the difference between a company's net sales and the cost of what it sold. *Gross Profit Margin* (or *Gross Profit Percentage*) is the ratio of the gross profit to the net sales. So, for example, if a store buys a widget for $1.00 (cost) and sells it for $1.50, its gross profit is 50 cents and its gross profit percentage is 33.3% (0.50/1.50).

$$Gross\ Profit\ Margin\ =\ \frac{Gross\ Profit}{Net\ Sales}$$

A company's gross profit margins, *within the context of the industry the company operates in*, are an indicator of the acceptance in the marketplace of the company's products or services. Comparing the gross profit margin of two companies in the same business will suggest differences in how valuable each company's products are judged to be by customers. A high amount of **added value** in a company's products or services that comes from features like better performance or longer durability and from cosmetic features usually yields higher gross profit margins than products without those features.

Importantly, the trend of a company's gross profit margin can be a clue to how customers' opinions of its products are changing. A company whose gross profit margins are holding steady or improving is likely to be able to keep growing its net profit, too, particularly if its sales are also growing. Net profit margins that aren't keeping in step deserve an explanation. Management's explanations of any unexpected changes in the gross profit margin from period to period can help you understand if the changes are temporary or likely to be long-lived and whether they signal a trend in the market for the company's products.

$$Net\ Profit\ Margin\ =\ \frac{Net\ Earnings}{Net\ Sales}$$

This would be a good time to return to Fossil's current 10-K report *and* current 10-Q report to familiarize yourself with both the current net sales trend and gross profit margin results. Compare the current annual numbers with the 5-year trends and the current quarterly numbers with the same quarter of last year for meaning and context. A comparison of Fossil's gross profit margin and the other companies in its industry group is available in the "key statistics" section at Fidelity's website and others. As said before, comparison with other similar companies and comparison of trends over time are more important than stand-alone statistics.

The first bit of financial analysis done and you're still standing. I said you could do it, and you did it.

Efficiency and Liquidity

The term "efficiency" is often used in connection with a process much as "productivity" is used in connection with work to describe output per cost unit of labor. It is also an appropriate term to use to describe a company's profitability in relation to the cost of its investment in its assets, its capital.

One way to evaluate a company's efficiency is to examine the returns statistics, including return on investment, return on assets and return on equity. These statistics are usually provided at your broker's research pages on the website. You will recall that your original screening thresholds to qualify a suspect as a prospect included return on equity and return on investment. However, the return statistics don't reveal much about *why* one company generates one return on investment value while another similar company generates a significantly different return on investment.

Company managers determine the most efficient use of capital based on the demands of the business. This involves making intelligent decisions about expenditures for fixed assets such as real estate, machinery, equipment and fixtures, and implementing sound policies to manage accounts receivable and inventory.

One way to form an opinion of how well management is doing in this regard is to calculate the annual *turnover* rates of major asset categories, and to compare those statistics to those of similar companies and to compare the company's turnover statistics from period to period.

A company's Balance Sheet breaks down the assets into two major categories: **current assets** and **long-term**, or **fixed**, **assets**. A company's current assets – those assets that are either cash or are likely to be converted into cash within one year – include primarily its accounts receivable and inventory, in addition to its cash. The Balance Sheet also lists the company's current liabilities which are obligations that are due for payment within one year. The difference between the current assets and the current liabilities is termed **net working capital**. Long-term assets refer to a company's investment in machinery, equipment, fixtures, as well as its investments in intangible assets like goodwill.

Accounts Receivable

A company's *accounts receivable* result from credit sales to customers with payment due sometime after the order is fulfilled. Receivables are constantly being created from sales and payments are constantly being received. The outstanding accounts receivable at any one time represent the credit sales that have not yet been collected. Hopefully the accounts receivable that existed at the beginning of the year have all been collected by the end of the year (or, if not collected, written off) and have been replaced by receivables that have been created by new sales during the year. The *accounts receivable turnover rate* reveals how many times a year this cycle occurs in full. A faster turnover rate is better because it reflects a faster conversion of sales into cash, and thus a lesser need for capital. The turnover rate is affected by several attributes: the average terms of sale, the level of customer claims and disputes, the nature and creditworthiness of the customer base, and how well the credit and collection function is managed.

It can be difficult to evaluate the quality of the accounts receivable based solely on the turnover, especially if your company sells to a variety of customer types – some for cash and some on credit terms. Any major change in the mix of cash and credit sales from year to year will distort the turnover numbers and so a trend toward faster turnover may reflect only a mix tilting toward cash sales and say nothing about the quality of the receivables. The opposite is also true: slowing turnover may reflect a mix of business tilting toward more credit sales and not deterioration in customer creditworthiness, disputation or poor credit management. But slower-turning accounts receivable may in fact indicate deterioration in their quality and, if true, would suggest that earnings might be overstated by some amount. A negative trend should be investigated. In any event, for purposes of evaluating the efficiency of capital, the turnover ratio is a reliable measure.

To calculate the turnover of accounts receivable, add the accounts receivable from the current fiscal year-end Balance Sheet to the accounts receivable amount on the previous year's Balance Sheet and divide the sum by 2 to obtain the average accounts receivable. Then divide the current year's net sales by the average accounts receivable number to obtain the accounts receivable turnover rate in times per year.

$$\text{Accounts Receivable Turnover} = \frac{\text{Net Sales}}{\substack{\text{Average of Two Successive Year-end} \\ \text{Accounts Receivables Values}}}$$

This process can be enhanced with just one more simple calculation: divide 365 by the turnover rate to obtain the turnover rate in days or **average days sales outstanding** (DSO). This number will be used later to calculate the **cash conversion cycle**.

$$\text{Days Sales Outstanding (DSO)} = \frac{365}{\text{Accounts Receivable Turnover}}$$

Inventory

A company's inventory is constantly in the process of being sold and simultaneously being replenished with new inventory. *Inventory turnover* tells us how many times a year the cycle occurs in full. Again, the more times inventory turns in a year, the less capital is required.

You may have heard the expression "just in time" inventory. It refers to a strategy designed to shorten the time between the acquisition of inventory and its sale. In a manufacturing setting, this refers to raw materials and components being received as close as possible to the time they are put into the production of finished goods. In a retail environment, finished goods are received from the manufacturer as close as possible to the time they are displayed in the store for sale to customers and as close to the time of year customers are likely to buy them. The key benefit of "just in time" inventory strategies is the efficient use of capital. A residual benefit is the lower cost involved in storing and insuring a smaller inventory. The risk of "just in time" strategies is that any interruption in the flow of goods can have severe negative consequences for manufacturing efficiencies, sales and customer service.

In a business that deals in inventory, whether as a producer, wholesaler or retailer, inventory should be a main focus of management's attention. Investors also need to pay very close attention to a company's inventory. Too much inventory puts strain on capital resources. The wrong inventory means customers' needs can't be satisfied at proper gross profit margins. Problems with inventory can be tied to many business failures, particularly in industries where seasonality and obsolescence factors are at play.

Monitoring trends in a company's inventory turnover rate, in addition to revealing how efficiently capital is being utilized, can alert us to possible problems. A slowdown in the turnover of inventory can be an early sign that some inventory may be old, past the main selling season, out of style or obsolete. In such a case, future gross profit margins may be headed downward as out-of-date or obsolete inventory is liquidated at lower prices. An inventory slowdown may also indicate problems in managing and executing the basic functions of the business. If management has admitted to having inventory issues in the past, monitoring the turnover in subsequent periods can indicate to what extent the problems are being corrected.

To calculate inventory turnover, go to the Balance Sheet and add together the inventory figure at the current year-end and the inventory number at the end of the previous year and then divide by 2 to obtain the average inventory. Then obtain "cost of sales" or "cost of goods sold" from the current year's Income Statement and divide that number by the average inventory number to obtain the inventory turnover rate in times per year.

$$\text{Inventory Turnover} = \frac{\text{Cost of Goods Sold}}{\text{Average of Two Successive Year-end Inventory Values}}$$

To express the turnover as **days of inventory outstanding** (DIO), simply divide 365 by the turnover rate in times per year. Stay tuned to learn how we use DIO and DSO to determine a company's cash conversion cycle.

$$\text{Days Inventory Outstanding (DIO)} = \frac{365}{\text{Inventory Turnover}}$$

Note: Your broker's "key statistics" section of its research webpages may well include turnover figures for both accounts receivable and inventory. You are welcome to refer to those if you want to be quick about it, but my guess is that if you've gotten through the book this far, you would prefer to rely on yourself for most of this easy stuff. The turnover numbers at the website are valuable if there is a comparison between the company you're analyzing and the medians for its industry group, as the comparison gives you some context to the raw numbers.

Cash Conversion Cycle

Accounts receivable and inventory turnover rates, taken together, can be used to calculate a company's *cash conversion cycle* – an estimate of the number of days it takes for cash that leaves the business to purchase and produce goods to be returned to the company. The cycle begins with the purchase of raw materials or finished goods. In a manufacturing company, labor and overhead (costs of plant managers, factory maintenance, depreciation of equipment, etc.) are added to raw materials for processing into a finished product. Inventory on a manufacturer's Balance Sheet includes materials in the raw state, work in process of becoming a finished good, and in the finished goods. When the finished goods are sold, the company either receives cash from its cash customers or it records on its books an account receivable due from its credit customers, with cash expected to be received some number of days after the sale.

The time it takes for a purchase to be converted into cash includes the time spent as inventory plus the time spent as a receivable. You just learned how to calculate accounts receivable and inventory turnover. Before determining the cash conversion cycle one more simple arithmetic calculation is needed to account for the fact that a company's suppliers may grant credit terms that allow it to delay payment for some number of days after it has received the inventory.

To calculate the cash conversion cycle, first return to the current year's and previous year's Balance Sheets to find the numbers for "accounts payable." Combine the two amounts and then divide the sum by 2 to determine the average accounts payable. Divide the "cost of goods sold" for the current year (from the Income Statement) by the average accounts payable to determine accounts payable turnover *times*.

$$Accounts\ Payable\ Turnover = \frac{Cost\ of\ Goods\ Sold}{Average\ of\ Two\ Successive\ Year\text{-}end\ Accounts\ Payables\ Values}$$

Then divide 365 by accounts payable turnover *times* to determine accounts payable turnover expressed in *days* (DPO).

$$Days\ Payables\ Outstanding\ (DPO) = \frac{365}{Accounts\ Payable\ Turnover}$$

Now calculate the cash conversion cycle by adding the DSO and DIO together and subtracting the DPO.

$$Cash\ Conversion\ Cycle = DSO + DIO - DPO$$

By looking at a company's major trading accounts of inventory, accounts receivable and accounts payable together, the cash conversion cycle gives us a sense of not only how efficiently capital is being utilized currently but also of the company's *liquidity* – its ability to pay its day in and day out costs and expenses as they come due. The shorter the cash conversion cycle is the less net working capital is needed to fund the company today and the less net working capital is required to support future growth. Some businesses, like restaurants, can operate quite successfully with very little net working capital because they typically get credit terms from their suppliers (although the terms are quite short), their inventory turns quickly and virtually all of their sales are for cash or convertible into cash in a day or two. As with most financial statistics and ratios, the most value from analyzing a company's cash conversion cycle is obtained by comparing one company to other similar companies and by comparing changes in a company's cycle from year to year.

Long-term, or Fixed, Assets

Long-term assets don't actually "turn over" in the way accounts receivable and inventories do. They are not typically acquired, sold and replaced during a year's time. Rather, long-term assets are constantly being used and reused in the operation of the business. How efficiently they are used can be inferred by their turnover rate.

Consider two fishermen. Fisherman A owns an old 14-foot aluminum boat with a 20-horsepower motor that he bought at an auction for $500. He has a $50 spinning reel and a $20 rod, and every morning he goes down to the lake and spends 5 hours fishing for walleye which he sells at the dock to a processor. Fisherman B owns a $12,000 18-foot boat with a 120-horsepower motor. He fishes with a $500 bait casting reel mounted on a $100 rod, and every morning he goes down to the same lake and fishes for walleye for 5 hours. Both fishermen keep track of every fish they catch for the whole season. At the end of the season, each man has caught 500 walleye weighing a total of 1,000 pounds. Assign an arbitrary sale value of $5.00 to each pound of fish and it is pretty easy to conclude that Fisherman A's operation, which involved a $570 investment in equipment that produced $5,000 of sales (a turnover of almost 9 times), made much more efficient use of its investment than did Fisherman B's operation with its $12,600 investment, whose turnover was only 0.4 times. That's not to say that Fisherman B, if he had fished longer hours, perhaps on a better fishing lake and with greater skill, could not have produced a lot more fish than Fisherman A. But the fact is that he didn't, so his investment in equipment was used much less efficiently than Fisherman A's investment.

One could conclude that the two fisherman were equally-skilled in the art of fishing but that Fisherman A was the wiser capitalist.

Just as we compared the operations of two fishermen, comparing turnover rates between two companies can help us decide which might make the better investment. And comparing turnover rates from one year to the next can give us a clue to issues affecting our prospect. A slowdown in a company's long-term asset turnover rate may be a result of declining sales, which usually result in declining earnings, which would likely also be reflected in a declining return on assets. A slowdown in the turnover rate may also be a result of a big acquisition or a series of smaller acquisitions or expansions which have not yet resulted in a correspondingly large increase in revenue. A slowdown may also reflect poor decision-making by management whose investments aren't producing the sales they expected or a change in the business where more frequent upgrading of facilities is a response to new competitive pressures. In any case, an increase in fixed assets relative to sales is an indicator that capital is being used less efficiently and that dynamic detracts from the company's investment appeal.

The numbers you need to calculate the turnover of fixed assets are found in the financial statements in the company's annual report on form 10-K. Divide net sales by long-term assets (from the Balance Sheet, subtract total current assets from total assets to determine long-term assets). This simple arithmetic reveals how efficiently the entire net investment in non-current assets was used to produce revenue for the company.

$$\text{Fixed Asset Turnover} = \frac{\textit{Net Sales}}{\textit{Total Assets} - \textit{Total Current Assets}}$$

It's time to return to your examination of Fossil. From the information on the financial statements in the 10-K, calculate its long-term asset turnover rate and its cash conversion cycle. Then, to give the numbers some meaning, go back to Section I of the 10-K report and try to relate how the company does business to the turnover numbers, noting particularly the "who, what, where and how" of its product sourcing and sales. Spend a while speculating how possible changes in the way Fossil's business is conducted would likely affect turnover statistics.

If, while you've got your eyes glued to Fossil's 10-K report, someone looks over your shoulder and asks what you're doing, tell them, "Oh, just some fundamental analysis." Watch their expression. Congratulations...it's a good bet that you've already done more fundamental financial analysis than your financial advisor does before he or she recommends an investment.

Solvency and Sustainability

This is the final section of the chapter on due diligence. If you have kept your suspect on your prospect list up to this point, you have learned a great deal about its business. Its rate of growth and its returns have met your thresholds. You understand how it does business, have some appreciation for the quality of its management and have a sense of how customers accept its products or services. You must have some positive feelings about the sustainability of what you believe has been a good track record or you would have scratched it from your prospect list by now. The *enterprising investor* part of your personality is probably pretty well satisfied that this prospect represents an attractive investment opportunity.

What's left is evaluating whether or not the company has the financial health and muscle to carry out its business strategy and to stay out of financial trouble for the foreseeable future. This is a primary concern of the *defensive investor* part of your personality – a concern that the company will fail to deliver on its potential because it has run short of capital and is not in a position to get more. It is also the primary concern of the company's lenders and other creditors, and if they would not want to lend money to a company, you probably don't want to buy common stock in it. It will be helpful to look at your prospect in much the same way a lender does and evaluate the company's solvency.

Salaries of employees, payment to vendors for purchases of inventory, services and supplies, payments to lenders of principal and interest, and payments to governments for taxes are all obligations that must ultimately be paid for in cash and on time. The parties listed all have the right to demand cash on the current day or on some day in the future from the company's supply of cash that exists on the day it is demanded. This section will focus on those attributes of a company's financial picture that affect both the demand for cash and the supply of cash.

The principal documents I recommend you use to evaluate a prospect's solvency are the Balance Sheet and the Income Statement, which are found in the annual 10-K report. Some readers may be surprised that I'm not going to refer them to the Statement of Cash Flows as well. I could, but I find the Statement of Cash Flows somewhat daunting for newer analysts and the Balance Sheets and Income Statements can provide a number of useful shortcuts.

If a company has absolutely no liabilities, it may fail to be successful and go out of business but it will never be insolvent, since insolvency requires that there be obligations that can't be paid. A lemonade stand isn't a likely candidate for bankruptcy. From that obvious point, we can make the assumption that even though debt or liabilities of one sort or another are necessary in any modern business, the less reliance a company has on debt the less likely it is that it will become insolvent. Of course, a term like "less" has to be relative to something in order to be meaningful, and a phrase like "relative to something" generally suggests that a ratio or two are involved. Thankfully, ratios are easy to calculate and comprehend or else this financial analysis stuff would be difficult, which it isn't.

To understand to what degree your prospect relies on debt to finance its business, take a look at its Balance Sheet, which amounts to a snapshot of the financial condition of the company as of the date of the financial statements. In the 10-K report, a list of company assets appears first, followed below by a list of liabilities and stockholders' equity.

Unlike the format in 10-K reports, in traditional presentations of business financial statements, the left hand side of the Balance Sheet lists all of the assets, or property, of the company and their estimated values as of the date of the financial statement. The right hand side lists all of the known liabilities of the company on that date. Starting at the top, the liabilities that come due within one year of the statement date are listed. These are labeled "current liabilities" and are subtotaled. Below the subtotal are listed the liabilities that are due for payment at some point after one year. These are labeled "long-term liabilities." The total of the current liabilities and the long-term liabilities represents the amount of money, or capital, outsiders have invested in the assets of the business. These outsiders are considered *creditors*. The total assets and total liabilities are never exactly the same amount. The difference between the two totals is also shown on the right hand side beneath the last liability listed, and is labeled "stockholders' equity." It is shown on the Balance Sheet so that the final totals on both sides are the same, or in *balance*. This arithmetic remainder represents the estimated amount of money the stockholders currently have invested in the assets of the company. Stockholders' equity has no due date and is sometimes referred to as the company's "book value."

There are a number of ratios that can be calculated that will relate the level of your prospect's debt to its assets, to its total capital, etc. All of them are useful, but unless you want to show off, it is sufficient to rely on the **debt to equity ratio** to determine the amount of financial *leverage* the company is employing. To calculate the debt to equity ratio, simply divide the total liabilities by stockholders' equity.

$$Debt\ to\ Equity\ Ratio = \frac{Current\ Liabilities + Long\text{-}term\ Liabilities}{Stockholders'\ Equity}$$

The smaller the ratio of debt to equity, the less the company is relying on debt that must be repaid. A small debt to equity ratio usually suggests that there is less risk of the company ultimately defaulting on its obligations to creditors and the greater the likelihood that the company will be able to sustain its operations over a long period of time. I prefer companies whose debt to equity ratio is not more than 1.0 to 1.0, meaning they have no more than one-half of their capital structure consisting of liabilities, including interest-bearing debt as well as non-interest bearing debt. That's an unreasonable threshold in some cases, I admit, particularly in certain industries like hospitality, casino operators, real estate investment trusts and utilities where the investment in long-term assets often far exceeds investments in working capital assets and where debt is primarily *very* long-term. There are always exceptions to guidelines and in those cases it is advisable to compare your prospect's ratios to those of other companies in the same industry.

The debt to equity ratio is important, but just as important is the ratio of debt to the amount of cash the company's operations generate each year that can be used to repay the debt. You can think of the amount of money available to repay debt as simply the amount of cash generated by the operations of the business that isn't used to invest in more assets. Financial analysts refer to it as *free cash flow*. Unless the company is going to increase the amount of money it owes to one creditor to reduce the amount of money it owes to another creditor, the means to repay debts has to come from the operation of the business. Otherwise, the burden of debt will increase and the risk of insolvency will increase.

The company's Income Statement, prepared according to *generally accepted accounting principles* (GAAP), does a pretty good job of estimating the costs and expenses of the business which are deducted from the company's sales to reveal the amount of net earnings. GAAP accounting for income involves *accrual accounting* which records revenue when it is earned and records costs and expenses when they are incurred, not when cash is actually received or spent. It even deducts non-cash items like depreciation as an expense even though the estimated loss of value of fixed assets over time (depreciation) doesn't involve cash at all. So, the Income Statement doesn't tell us how much cash the company generated or how much was spent or for what. Fortunately, the company's financial statements do include a Statement of Cash Flows which you could pore over at length to see where the money came from and where it went, but a quick shortcut will serve the purpose just fine.

There is a simple way to modify the GAAP Income Statement just for your purposes. You're not bound by any accounting rules and regulations if you're simply arranging numbers to help you understand what you want to understand. You can create a modified Income Statement that better reveals to what extent a company can repay its existing debts without piling on more liabilities and without depleting its cash. I use an admittedly conservative modification that reduces the net profit on the GAAP Income Statement by the amount of the growth in the company's investments in all assets except cash. The net result suggests to what extent the company can sustain itself without relying on additional capital. One could refer to my modified Income Statement as a *Sustainability Income Statement*.

Constructing a "Sustainability Income Statement" requires consulting the current year's Income Statement and the Balance Sheets from the current year and the previous year. All the numbers needed are in the financial statements section of the10-K report.

Step 1. From each of the two Balance Sheets, subtract the "Total Current Assets" subtotal from "Total Assets." Call the remainders "long-term assets current year" and "long-term assets previous year."

> *Total Assets current year*
> *– Total Current Assets current year*
> *Long-term Assets current year*

> *Total Assets previous year*
> *– Total Current Assets previous year*
> *Long-term Assets previous year*

Now subtract the "long-term assets previous year" number from the "long-term assets current year" number. This is your "*change* in long-term assets." (If the "long-term assets this year" number is less than the "long-term assets last year" number, record the negative "change" number.)

> *Long-term Assets current year*
> *– Long-term Assets previous year*
> *Change in Long-term Assets*

Step 2. From each Balance Sheet, subtract the assets labeled "cash," "marketable securities" and/or "short-term investments" from the "Total Current Assets" total. Call the remainders "non-cash current assets current year" and "non-cash current assets previous year."

> *Total Current Assets current year*
> *– Cash Assets current year*
> *Non-cash Current Assets current year*

> *Total Current Assets previous year*
> *– Cash Assets previous year*
> *Non-cash Current Assets previous year*

Now, subtract the "non-cash current assets previous year" number from the "non-cash current assets current year" number. This is your "*change* in non-cash current assets." (If the "non-cash current assets current year" number is less than the "non-cash current assets previous year" number, record the negative "change" number.)

> *Non-cash Current Assets current year*
> *– Non-cash Current Assets previous year*
> *Change in Non-cash Current Assets*

Step 3. Combine the values for "change in long-term assets" and "change in non-cash current assets." This sum represents the *net* new investments (after deducting accruals for depreciation and amortization) that the company made during the most recent year.

> *Change in Long-term Assets*
> *+ Change in Non-cash Current Assets*
> *Net New Investments*

Now deduct the "net new investments" from "Net Earnings" on the current year's Income Statement. Call the remainder "Sustainability Income."

> *Net Earnings*
> *– Net New Investments*
> *Sustainability Income*

The *Sustainability Income* of a company reflects the amount of GAAP earnings that was available to increase cash balances, reduce liabilities, pay dividends or buy back some outstanding stock in the company.

If the Net Earnings number on the GAAP Income Statement is a positive number but the Sustainability Income number is negative, it means that earnings during the period were insufficient to fund the increase in non-cash assets. In such a case, the net increase in total non-cash assets had to come from somewhere other than from earnings: either from a reduction in the amount cash on hand at the start of the year, an increase in liabilities, an increase in equity capital, or some combination of those sources.

Of course, a growing company invariably acquires more assets over time, especially current assets which are a function of growing sales. As sales grow, more inventory is required to fill orders and more accounts receivable are created by the higher level of sales. Investments in long term assets normally increase as the company expands its manufacturing or distribution capacity to handle the increased activity. And if a company grows through acquisition, so will its investment in intangible assets like goodwill. The investments in these long-term assets are often made in rather large "lumps" ahead of earnings, using borrowings to finance the outlays in anticipation of a payback from higher earnings.

So, if your prospect's Sustainability Income Statement shows a negative number from time to time, it is not necessarily a danger signal, especially if the company is a rather young one and is growing quickly. If it started out the year with a lot of cash or very few liabilities, there is probably no immediate problem. But it might be a danger signal if the negative numbers continue year after year, revealing an inability of the company to self-fund its operations. You will be well-advised to make sure you understand why the situation continues before committing your investment dollars. Reading management's discussion in the annual report and listening in on the conference calls may satisfy your concerns. If not, you are fully justified in not investing in the company.

You have probably heard at least once of some company that has used what is euphemistically called "creative accounting" to obscure the actual financial results of the company. It is sometimes called "cooking the books." Usually, such bad behavior overstates the company's earnings. Calculating Sustainability Income can sometimes detect the sleight of hand.

If a company's management wants to overstate profitability, accrual accounting can sometimes be an unwitting accomplice. That's because when it comes to asset values, fairly wide latitude is given to management estimates. This comes in handy for dishonest managers who might postpone taking reserves for obsolete inventory or uncollectible accounts receivable, for example, thereby overstating their values and overstating profits as reported by GAAP. But the Sustainability Income Statement deducts increases in the net amount of all assets except cash as if they were expenses and thus Sustainability Income is reduced, tending to frustrate the deception.

Management may fool their auditors and get away with deception the first time it is used. If so, it is likely that once management sees how easy such a sleight of hand was to execute, they will resort to it again and again. Eventually, an analyst will see a declining trend in cash flow or Sustainability Income caused by the inflated asset values and will start to ask questions of the company's managers. If the answers don't satisfactorily ease the analyst's concerns, he may publicly voice his concerns and cast doubt on the integrity of the financial reporting. His discomfort with the numbers may precipitate a loss of confidence in the company by investors. The stock price may tumble and investors may lose money. It is very difficult for a company's stock price to recover from such a series of events.

If you prepare a Sustainability Income Statement on each of your prospects before you invest, you may detect a problem early and avoid being a victim of creative accounting.

If your prospect's Sustainability Income is consistently a positive number, that's a good thing, because it indicates that the company is generating enough cash to sustain its current operations with some to spare. Ideally, the Sustainability Income should also be large enough to pay off a substantial portion of the company's debt if it was required to do so.

To determine how meaningful the company's Sustainability Income is to the level of its debts, you can calculate what portion of the debt could be repaid by the current year's Sustainability Income, or alternatively, how many years it would take to repay the debt. Here's how...

From the current year's financial statements, add up interest-bearing debt amounts which are found on the Balance Sheet. These will be identified as "notes payable," "short-term borrowings," "short-term debt," "current portion of long-term debt" and "long-term debt," or very similar descriptions. To determine how many years it would take to repay the company's interest-bearing debt, divide the total of those debt obligations by the Sustainability Income amount.

$$Debt\ Payback\ Period\ (years)\ =\ \frac{Total\ Interest\text{-}bearing\ Debt}{Sustainability\ Income}$$

I like to see a number less than 4 but, of course, every industry is different and capital-intensive businesses, like regulated utilities, carry huge amounts of long-term debt on their Balance Sheets and their payback periods may exceed 10 years.

If your prospect's payback period seems unreasonably long to you, you can either avoid the investment or you can compare it to other similar companies to see if your prospect's payback period is typical. And don't look just at the current year, which may be exceptionally good or exceptionally bad when it comes to producing Sustainability Income. A good analyst looks at trends over time and, in the case of Sustainability Income, seeing it follow in a nice upward trajectory similar to the trajectory of the reported GAAP earnings suggests a sustainable business worthy of your investment consideration.

Finally, Sustainability Income can provide you with a good sense of the company's ongoing ability to maintain or increase its dividend, which may be especially important to you if you are counting on dividends for some of your personal income. If Sustainability Income is about equal to or even less than the amount of the annual dividend amount, there is reason to feel skeptical that the current dividend level can be maintained. At a minimum, you want to see that the Sustainability Income amply covers the dividend amount. Here again, one year may not tell the whole story but by looking at a few recent years and understanding the trend, you can get a very good sense of how secure, or sustainable, the current dividend level is.

Calculating the ratio of Sustainability Income to the current annual dividend involves calculating "Sustainability Income Per Share." First determine the average number of shares outstanding during the year by combining the number of shares outstanding at the end of the current fiscal year and the number of shares outstanding at the end of the previous fiscal year, and then dividing by 2 to get the average. These amounts are found in the 10-K report on the company's Balance Sheet in the "Stockholders' Equity" section.

$$\textit{Average Outstanding Shares} = \frac{\textit{Outstanding Shares of Two Successive Years}}{2}$$

Then divide Sustainability Income by the average number of shares to determine "Sustainability Income Per Share."

$$\textit{Sustainability Income Per Share} = \frac{\textit{Sustainability Income}}{\textit{Average Outstanding Shares}}$$

Now divide the Sustainability Income Per Share by the amount of the annual dividend per share. The answer reveals a **coverage ratio**, which is the multiple of Sustainability Income over the dividend payment.

$$\textit{Dividend Coverage Ratio} = \frac{\textit{Sustainability Income Per Share}}{\textit{Annual Dividend Per Share}}$$

If your answer is greater than 1, then Sustainability Income *covers* the dividend. That's good as far as it goes but it doesn't totally assure you that there is money available to pay the entire dividend amount after making necessary debt repayments. What you want to see is a sizable cushion between the Sustainability Income and the dividend. That means the coverage ratio should be a number close to 2 or more, particularly if there is a fair amount of debt on the Balance Sheet and if the debt payback period you just calculated is fairly high. The higher the coverage ratio is, the higher the level of confidence that the dividend can be maintained or even increased, while comfortably paying back debts.

Note: Upgrading your understanding of a company's ability to maintain the amount of dividends it pays to common shareholders requires an understanding of two things: how much debt is coming due annually and, if the company has preferred stock outstanding, the amount of the required dividends on the preferred shares. These amounts can be found in the notes to the company's financial statements and should be deducted from the Sustainability Income amount before calculating the ratio of Sustainability Income to the annual dividend. I recommend you undertake the fine tuning step if your coverage ratio is less than 2.0 to 1 or if your debt payback period is greater than 4 years.

As the last step in your due diligence on Fossil, return to its most recent 10-K report and construct a Sustainability Income Statement for the current year and the previous year. Record your conclusion about the company's ability to repay its obligations or to pay dividends or buy back some of its outstanding stock.

Principle #7 – Go Heavy on the Crème de la Crème

You are well on your way to picking a company or two to buy. You have a lot of choices and you have the luxury of time in which to make your choice. There is no rush. It's natural for you to want to start putting your money to work as soon as possible. But don't forget that you're making what you hope is a long term investment, not a bet on the next spin of the roulette wheel or roll of the dice. I recommend that you always look at two or three companies in the same line of business and compare their growth, their returns, their strategies, their competitive advantages and their financial capacities. Then pick the one that is the very best of the bunch, the "crème de la crème," as one of my Heller colleagues was fond of saying. In other words, don't settle.

Principle #8 – Don't Overpay

One of the most important factors affecting the returns you will get from your stock investments is what you pay for them in the first place. If you pay too much for the stocks you buy, the returns you get will be less than they would be if you always paid a fair price…and a lot less than if you managed to buy some of them at bargain prices. The secret to making extraordinary returns is to buy your stocks for less than they are worth. And that requires that you have some idea of what they are worth.

Basic Valuation Principles

The price of a share of stock of a company is $1/n^{th}$ of the market value of the entire company, "n" being the total number of shares of the company that are outstanding. Companies issue shares and the market determines what the shares are valued at, thereby determining what the whole company is valued at. For example, if Company A issues 1 million shares and the market values each share at $20, then the whole company is valued at $20 million. If Company B issues 2 million shares and the market values each share at $10, then Company B also has a market value of $20 million. Either way, each is a $20 million "pie" sliced in two different ways. If you have $1,000 to invest, you could choose to buy 50 shares of Company A stock or you could buy twice as many shares of Company B stock. Either way, you have purchased $1,000 worth of stock and you own 0.005% of the company.

> Remember this: by itself, the price of a share of stock says nothing about whether it is an "expensive" stock or a "cheap" stock. If the price of a share of stock in Coca-Cola (KO) is going for $75 and the price of a share of stock in Pepsico (PEP) sells for $65, don't take that to mean that Pepsi's stock is less expensive than Coke's. It might be but it might not be. If the price of a share of Apple (AAPL) is priced at $600, don't assume it is more expensive than DELL (DELL) at $15. It might be but it might not be. Even though we have a natural tendency to be intimidated by big numbers, don't fall into that trap when it comes to share prices.

The following principles are important:

- The real, or intrinsic, value of a company to an investor is related to its earnings; not just its current earnings, but *all* of its future earnings.

- Since all of the future earnings of a company are important but unknowable, when investors compare the market value of a whole company or the price of a share of its stock to its earnings, they relate it to what is known: the earnings the company generated during the trailing twelve months.

The most common valuation statistic is the ***price-earnings ratio*** (***PE ratio***). This valuation ratio relates two known numbers: the most recent earnings per share to the current price per share. The arithmetic involves simply dividing the current price of one share of stock by the earnings per share for the trailing twelve months (TTM) to determine what *multiple* of earnings the stock price represents. (If you have misplaced your $2.99 calculator, you can find the PE ratio for your prospect by entering its symbol in the "quotes" box at any number of free sites like yahoo.com or from your broker. Fidelity's "detailed quote" option on its stock research screen includes the current PE ratio for the symbol you enter.)

For example, if Company A's shares are selling for $20 and reports $1.00 of earnings per share over the trailing twelve months, its stock is selling for a multiple of 20 times earnings or, as most commonly put, the company's stock has a PE ratio of 20. That means the investor can own $1/n^{th}$ of all of the company's earnings for the entire future of the company if she is willing to shell out $20 today and hold onto her share forever. Of course, no one knows how much those future earnings will amount to, but if Company A's future annual earnings per share never wavered from $1.00 she would have earned her $20 back over the next 20 years and still be entitled to her share of the company's future earnings – forever.

If you reverse the arithmetic and divide the earnings per share by the stock price, you will get an "EP" ratio of 1/20, or 5%. This valuation ratio is called ***earnings yield***. For an investor willing to accept an earnings yield of 5%, we can say that $1.00 of earnings per year forever has a value today, or ***present value***, of $20.00. (Don't confuse *earnings* yield with *dividend* yield.)

An investor demanding an earnings yield higher than 5% would not pay $20 for a share of Company A's stock. An investor demanding an earnings yield of 10%, for example, would value a share of Company A stock today at only $10. Said another way, he would not buy Company A's stock if the PE ratio was over 10.

> An investment earning 5% percent a year will double in value in approximately 14 years and an investment earning 10% a year will double in value in approximately 7 years. These are close approximations based on the "rule of 72," a shortcut that uses simple arithmetic to compare the effect of yields on the accumulation of wealth. Simply divide 72 by the yield rate to determine how many years it will take to double your money. Requiring a 10% earnings yield is reasonable for enterprising stock investors, based on long-term historical stock market returns.

But what if Company A's earnings, instead of being $1.00 a year forever, were expected to grow by 6% a year for the next 3 years before leveling off to a growth rate of just 2% a year, which happens to be the current targeted rate of inflation? That would justify a PE ratio somewhat higher than 10 to an investor seeking an earnings yield of at least 10%. He would be willing to pay something more than $10 per share because of the expected growth in earnings.

Determining what that higher PE ratio would be requires a calculation of present value (today's value) that uses a *discounted cash flow* formula, and that requires more horsepower than came with my $2.99 calculator. Fortunately there are a couple of easy ways to avoid buying a more expensive calculator or resorting to Excel. **Note:** In the online tools described here, the discount rate is the same as the earnings yield rate of 10%.

- A back-of-the-envelope calculation (actually, no envelope is required – it can be done in your head in a few seconds) – takes the "no-growth" PE of 10 and adds one-half the expected growth rate of 6 to arrive at an approximate PE of 13. This shortcut isn't precise but it is close enough to indicate if the current PE ratio of your prospect is anywhere in the ball park of what you might be willing to pay.

The Duly Diligent Stock Investor

- Among the extraordinarily valuable tools available online – for free – are several websites that provide interactive calculators that allow us to more precisely determine present value based on discounted cash flow analysis. Here are a couple:

  The calculator at

  moneychimp.com/articles/valuation/pe_ratio.htm

  gives you a reasonable PE ratio based on the growth you expect and your required earnings yield (discount rate). I entered the numbers from the Company A example and the calculator returned a "fair" PE ratio of 14.20, not far off the 13 resulting from the back-of-the-envelope calculation.

  The "price check" calculator at

  smartmoney.com/pricecheck

  is helpful because it supplies you with your prospect's earnings per share when you input the stock symbol. Based on your inputs this calculator returns net present value along with the recent price your stock traded at.

As these calculators reveal, the price earnings ratio of a company is a statement about the market's expectations of its future earnings and a higher PE ratio reflects an expectation of relatively greater *growth* in earnings.

It's certain that other investors and analysts are performing the same sort of calculations to come up with a "right" price, so you may be tempted to conclude that all stocks are fairly priced at all times. If that were true, you could just not worry about overpaying and buy your shares at whatever the market price is on the day you happened to place your order. Of course, we know that's not reality since the price of a share changes from day to day and from minute to minute within a day.

Gyrating stock prices typically have little to do with the fundamentals of the company whose stock is being bought and sold. A good bit of the daily change in stock prices occurs because of decisions made by large institutional investors (mutual funds and hedge funds) who are simply speculating on what other traders will be doing with their money in the near future. To be fair, some price movement is caused by fund managers who are adjusting the make-up of their portfolios, moving some of their investments into or out of industry sectors or individual companies as they attempt to enhance the performance of their investment funds. Sometimes they are reacting to economic news of one sort or the other, increasing their concentrations in segments that will likely benefit by whatever dynamic made the news and decreasing their concentrations in segments less likely to benefit from it.

A single institution making only minor portfolio adjustments wouldn't by itself affect the price of a stock all that much. But analysts and portfolio managers tend to have read most of the same books and to have attended the same seminars and one institutional investor's so-called "wisdom" is likely to be shared by a large number of his counterparts. So, when the portfolio managers of a number of large institutions tweak their portfolios even a little bit, they can collectively cause a big change in the price of the stock of one or even hundreds of companies. In sectors where there are more buyers and fewer sellers, the share prices go up. Where there are more sellers and fewer buyers, share prices go down. These movements in stock prices typically tend to go in the same direction for several days or even weeks, because the professionals tend to stealthily enter and exit their positions in rather small increments over time in an effort to avoid causing big, sudden changes in prices.

Even worse, a significant portion of daily trading is done by predetermined instructions entered into computers, involving triggers that send buy orders or sell orders to the brokerages. When a computer is programmed to make a trade, it is often reacting to a trade that another computer at another hedge fund made. For example, a computer at Fund A may be instructed to sell a certain number of shares in a company if the price falls by a certain amount. When Fund B's computer detects a large order at that lower price, it may have been instructed to react by selling its shares at the market price. When computers act without knowing or caring why a price has changed they have the potential for disturbing the whole market, at least for a time.

That's when the little investor (that's us) feels that he is being whipsawed; that Wall Street isn't playing fair; that he doesn't have a chance, especially when the prices of his stocks take a big hit for no apparent reason. I know that feeling and it's not a good one. I like it better when all of my stocks go up in price. It's then that I get the feeling that I went to bed smart and woke up a genius.

By the way, the professionals love it when you get the feeling that you don't have a chance up against the big Wall Street traders and speculators. They forget you're not playing their game; you're investing for your future. You want your company's earnings – forever. Don't forget that your long-term horizon, the due diligence you've performed and your use of a present value approach to determining a fair price should give you a measure of confidence in the face of the inevitable market gyrations.

Once you have done your due diligence and calculated a reasonable PE ratio and a fair price for your prospect, you will compare your fair price to the market price.

> Take a break from reading and, using the information you have gathered about FOSL to form an opinion about its future growth prospects, calculate a fair price for a share of its stock. Now compare the current market price of a share to your fair value calculation. Are the numbers close? Would this be a stock you would consider investing in and, if so, at what price?

Ideally, if you decide to buy, you will purchase your shares at some amount less than the fair price, providing you with a cushion or, as Warren Buffett calls it, a *margin of safety*. The cushion acts as both a hedge against the possibility of losing money and also as an enhancement to the amount of money you will ultimately make by owning the stock. Ideally, the price you pay for your shares should be 15-20% below fair value.

If the current price of the stock is higher than your determination of fair value, you should consider waiting to buy shares until

- The price of the stock has come down to below fair value and there has been no apparent negative change in the growth expectations of the company or in its competitive strengths, solvency or liquidity. (In other words, the *fundamentals* have not changed for the worse.) Stock prices move up and down over time in a ***trading range*** and your prospect's stock may be in the upper end of its trading range. You may have to wait quite a long while for the price to come down, especially if the stock market indexes are moving higher, keeping the price of your prospect's shares high. It is worth the wait. Stock prices do go on sale. The time when you are most likely to be able to get your shares at a better than fair price is when the major indexes have dropped and taken shares of your prospects down with them. It takes some fortitude to be a contrarian and buy when others are selling, but knowing what your business is worth lets you recognize an opportunity and take advantage of it.

- You have satisfied yourself that the company's fundamentals have improved; that is, it is growing faster than expected, its future looks brighter, and an honest fair value calculation indicates a higher price is justified. Be careful though: it is tempting to rationalize reasons for overpaying for your shares. Be honest with yourself and, as Davy Crockett said, "Be always sure you're right – then go ahead."

If the current price of your prospect's stock is *less* than what you've calculated its fair value to be you have only to do a few things before making your investment:

- Double check your assumptions. Take a fresh look at anything that may have bothered you a bit during the due diligence process. This is particularly advisable if your prospect's stock has been moving down while the major market indexes have been moving up. Normally, "a rising tide lifts all boats" but if your prospect's stock isn't being lifted, there might be something you're overlooking. If your stock has been moving down at all, don't be in a hurry to place your order. You may miss an opportunity to buy at the absolute bottom but that's to be expected. Identifying the precise bottom or top is almost always a matter of luck. Check the news for any negative press before committing. Make sure you have the most current quarterly reports and have reviewed them for any signs that the business is deteriorating. Davy Crockett's advice applies here as well.

- Up until now, I haven't recommended that you consult the analysts because this book has been about *you* being the analyst. For one thing, Wall Street analysts tend to serve traders and market-timers and they issue frequent "sells, "buys" and "holds." Worse yet, two analysts may publish opposite recommendations on the same day. Very confusing. Still, this is a proper time to "ask an expert," like the option given to contestants on the old TV game show, *Who Wants to Be a Millionaire?*. (You do want to be a millionaire, right?) Your broker's research section of the website will give you access to several research reports and you can get a host of opinions on yahoo.com, money.msn.com, seekingalpha.com and many more sites. Ultimately, it's your opinion that counts but checking out the opinions of others can be helpful, especially if you do so only after you've done your own due diligence and have reached your own conclusion.

Some of the risk of owning stocks is the **market risk**, the risk that the market will price stocks lower today and for a while into the future than it priced them yesterday. The bigger risk is the **company risk**, the risk that your company doesn't perform as you expected.

There is no reason for wringing hands or gnashing teeth over making a stock purchase. Don't let yourself be a victim of paralysis by analysis. Remember, you're about to invest in a good company that you have researched. Your due diligence has mitigated much of the company risk and your margin of safety has mitigated much of the market risk. And time mitigates much of both. Time is on your side and even if you do make a mistake and pay a little too much, you are likely to do just fine over time. I'm quite sure that folks who paid a little too much for Walmart shares in 1988 (I picked that year at random) have done just fine by 2012. You may not latch onto another Walmart growth story and you may not have 25 years left to wait but you get my point: having a long-term horizon mitigates a good part of the risk of paying a little too much.

If you're still hesitant, you can mitigate the risk of paying too much by accumulating your shares in increments over time. Buying your shares in two or more **tranches** (a fancy bizword for "chunks") spaced apart over several weeks or months can smooth out the price swings. You don't have to go off the high dive. You can wade into the water.

When it comes time to place your order, your brokerage account will give you several types of orders to choose from. Your broker's website and representatives can explain the various types of orders and the order entry process. The two main order choices are *market orders* and *limit orders*. If you specify a market order, you will buy shares at or near the quoted price of the stock at the time your order is received. Usually market orders are executed almost instantaneously. If you specify a limit order, you tell the broker the price per share you are willing to pay for the shares you want to buy. You will set your limit price at or below the market price, because you don't want to pay more than the market price. You will be asked to set an expiration date for the limit order, which could be the end of the current day or a date in the future.

Whichever order option you choose, you should be aware of some dates that can be important, especially where dividends are involved:

- *Transaction Date* is the date your order to buy (or sell) shares is executed.

- *Settlement Date* is the third business day after the transaction date. If your order is executed on Monday, your ownership is considered recorded on the company's books on Thursday.

Several dates are important when it comes to the payment of dividends.

- *Dividend Declaration Date* is the date the company announces to the public that it is going to pay a cash dividend on the *dividend payment date* only to stockholders appearing on the company's list of stockholders on the *record date*. For example, Company A may issue a press release on May 20 (the Declaration Date) that it will pay a 10 cent per share dividend on June 23 (the Payment Date) to stockholders of record on June 2 (the Record Date).

- *Ex-Dividend Date* is the date that the stock trades without that dividend. In other words, unless your order to buy shares is executed one or more days before the ex-dividend date, you will not be paid the upcoming dividend. In order to receive the upcoming dividend your order must be executed at least three days prior to the record date, which is the same as saying your transaction date must be at least one day prior to the ex-dividend date.

Caution: There is often a drop in the price of the stock on the ex-dividend date, reflecting the fact that buyers on that date won't be entitled to receive the dividend. If the dividend is a small amount relative to the stock price, this drop probably won't be significant and may not happen at all. But if a high-yield stock is involved, the drop is likely to get your attention. If you are surprised by a sudden drop in the share price, check the detailed quote page on your broker's website. It will show the ex-dividend date and may explain the change in the stock price.

Principle #9 – Diversify, But Not Too Much

A basic theory of investing is that risk of loss or poor performance is reduced by spreading the risks over multiple investments. Most investment advisors recommend that your financial investments be allocated to several kinds of investment, with some money going into stocks, some into bonds, some into real estate and perhaps some into commodities. The theory is that different types of investment perform differently at different times and that a diversified portfolio of investments delivers steadier returns and involves less risk of loss. Over time, diversification should produce superior results than a portfolio where risk is concentrated in just one type of investment. This is sound advice.

Within the portion of your investments that you decide to commit to common stocks, there should also be a spread of risk because you don't want to let a single mistake inflict a devastating blow to your goal of creating wealth for yourself. Protecting yourself from a *concentration* of risk involves building a portfolio that includes investments in several companies in several different industries.

A person with limited funds to invest may start out like my friend Jim and I did back in 1968 when we invested a small amount of money in each of two companies, Brunswick Corp. and American National Bank, which were in completely different lines of business. Investing in two companies doesn't provide much of a spread of risk but it does cut your concentration in half. If your funds available for investing are very limited but you have a plan to grow them, it would be a good idea to accumulate the funds over time in a low-cost index mutual fund. While you are accumulating funds, you can be researching and tracking your suspects and prospects so that when you've built up a meaningful balance, you will be ready to redirect some money from your mutual fund into investments in companies you want to own.

The same strategy can apply if you already have money in stock mutual funds that you would like to redirect into your own companies. Withdrawing a portion of your funds a little at a time and methodically building a portfolio would allow you to maintain a spread of risk as you perform your due diligence and select the crème de la crème you want to invest in.

How many stocks you should own in order to effectively limit your downside risk is a matter of debate and your tolerance for risk. I believe that the more stocks you own, the more your portfolio is likely to perform like the stock market as a whole. In other words, the more stocks you own the less your portfolio is exposed to individual company downside risk (and upside reward) and the more it is exposed to market risk and reward.

In order to strike a balance between your desire for your portfolio to grow faster than the market indexes while at the same time limiting your downside risk, you need to accept the risks inherent in having your investments in a relatively small number of companies. If you are retired and depend on your investment returns to cover your cost of living, you are naturally more risk averse than a younger investor with a secure job might be and so you are likely to take comfort in having a relatively large number of companies in your stock portfolio. (Do you recall Paul's Principle #1?) Also, being retired should give you more time to monitor the performances of your portfolio companies, allowing you to own more of them.

Even with time on your hands, I don't see much benefit in having a portfolio of more than 20 stocks for most people. I favor a portfolio of 8-15 well-chosen, solid companies purchased at a discount to estimated present value and representing at least 4 or 5 different business sectors and different industries within those sectors. Ideally, the industries represented in your portfolio should have little or no correlation to each other. By that I mean that they should not all be subject to the same economic factors to the same degree. For example, the restaurant industry is affected by the cost of food to a much larger degree than are the technology industries. Likewise, companies in the non-durable consumer industries are adversely affected by high energy prices and, of course, companies in the oil business are positively affected.

You can easily determine your prospect's sector and industry at finance.yahoo.com. Enter the company's stock symbol to find its sector and industry designation. Yahoo! also provides a listing of industries and sectors and an index of companies within each industry. The index can also be a source of suspects for you in case you have run out of your own ideas.

Principle #10 – Keep Score and Be Patient

Your brokerage account is going to provide you with the record keeping you will need to monitor the market value of your investments. The market value of your investments is continually being updated in real time, available for you to check whenever you get the urge. You'll likely be one of those investors who make daily visits to their broker's website to see how much money they "made" or "lost" that day, even though monitoring the stock price reveals nothing about how well a company's operations performed that day. Frequent visits to your broker's website can contribute to excessive (and expensive) trading, and that is not a good thing. Individual investors have a tendency to sell low and buy high based on emotion and that usually guarantees that they will lose money. Frequent trading is a symptom of that tendency.

A more beneficial way of monitoring the performance of your investments is to track the growth in earnings per share and the growth in the book value per share of each of your companies. You can do that on a free downloadable form you can get at **dulydiligent.com**, my publisher's web site. Scan the following QR code to go directly to the website:

Developing your own Excel worksheet or using old-fashioned ledger paper you can buy at an office supply store is fine too.

The discipline of tracking the financial progress of each of your companies instead of just monitoring how the stock is doing on the stock exchange forces you to think like a business owner. It alerts you to changes in how your companies are performing and helps you spot trends. You can compare these trends to the trends in the market price of your shares and seek to reconcile any diverging trends.

When your company's financial trends deteriorate, you'll decide if it is still where you want your money to be invested. If its future seems less bright than when you bought your shares, you can sell some or all of them. The more you consult your own form or spreadsheet, and the less you consult the daily gyrations of the stock prices, the more you will be demonstrating that you are a patient, savvy investor, not a nervous speculator.

Over my 25-year career as a lender, I experienced the inevitable reality that all lenders experience: not every extension of credit works out the way it was intended. When loans don't get paid back, you lose money. My goal was to extend the maximum amount of credit with a reasonable amount of loss. Our Heller business group expected to have losses and we budgeted for them but our losses were small because of the due diligence we did up front and the amount of attention we gave to our accounts.

Equity investing is similar: some of your investments will not perform as you expect and the market price of some of your stocks will drop below the price you paid. A drop in the market price doesn't necessarily mean you've lost real money though because market prices always fluctuate. As I noted above, the most certain way to guarantee a loss for yourself is to sell your stock in a good company for the sole reason that the market price has gone down. I've made some mistakes and held onto some of my investments longer than I should have and then sold for a loss that was more than it should have been but that hasn't happened too often. Usually a downward trend in the stock price reverses direction and over time the market price for superior companies recovers. The truth is I have erred in selling shares too early much more often than in selling shares too late, thereby missing out on big gains. Your initial due diligence and your continual monitoring are so important: knowing that you own a superior company and tracking its financial performance, and not just its stock price, will serve to minimize poor selling decisions. On the other hand, when deterioration in the company's performance is detected, when you question if the company is still superior and when the explanations you get from management don't inspire confidence in the company's future, you are fully justified in selling your shares – even if it means admitting that you made a mistake and that your mistake has cost you some money. Providing you the ability to quickly put your mistakes behind you is why Wall Street exists.

Principle #11 – Stay Humble

If the information you've obtained in this book has given you enough confidence to begin to identify some suspects, convert several of them to prospects and convert a few prospects into profitable investments, then I'm happy to have helped you get started. If this is the first book you have read about investing in stocks, let it be just the start of your education. I encourage you to seek out the wisdom of investing icons like Benjamin Graham, Warren Buffett and Peter Lynch, to name a few. Expanding your understanding of businesses, accounting principles, economics and financial analysis can be an interesting and rewarding endeavor.

Hopefully over time you will see big payoffs from the duly diligent investing you have taken the time to do. If at some point you find that your portfolio is beating most of the mutual funds, don't be surprised. You're being rewarded for your efforts. Be careful not to become overconfident though. Don't convince yourself that you can cut corners and replace duly diligent investing with seat-of-the-pants investing. Stay disciplined and stay humble.